SAVORING INDIA

Discovering the Richness of India's Culinary Heritage with Street Food and Royal Delights | Full Color Edition

Cristi G. Piedra

Manufactured in the United States of America
Interior and Cover Designer: Danielle Rees
Art Producer: Brooke White
Editor: Aaliyah Lyons
Production Editor: Sienna Adams
Production Manager: Sarah Johnson
Photography: Michael Smith

TABLE OF CONTENTS

TABLE OF CONTENTS

TABLE OF CONTENTS

INTRODUCTION

The essence of an Indian kitchen transcends borders, finding a home in kitchens around the globe. For me, it's right here in the heart of the United States. Growing up with a mix of Indian and American cultures, I've always felt a strong connection to my Indian roots, especially through food. My mom, who is from India, has been my guide on a flavorful journey that spans continents and generations.

My love for Indian cuisine started at home. I remember watching my mom effortlessly create dishes that filled our house with rich, aromatic spices. Every meal was a celebration of flavors, each bite was a reminder of our heritage. Despite being miles away from India, our kitchen was a portal to its vibrant culinary traditions.

I travel to my mom's hometown in India for two weeks every two years. These trips are like culinary pilgrimages, where I immerse myself in the local flavors and techniques. I watch, learn, and then bring these authentic tastes back to my kitchen in the U.S.

My mom's kitchen in India is a treasure trove of recipes passed down through generations. From simple, comforting dal to complex, aromatic biryanis, each dish tells a story of tradition and love. I cherish these moments in the kitchen with my mom, as they connect me to my Indian heritage in a profound way.

Back home, I try to recreate these flavors as best as I can. I visit local markets, seeking out spices and ingredients that mirror those I find in India. Cooking has become a way for me to bridge the gap between my two cultures, creating dishes that honor my heritage while embracing my American upbringing.

My kitchen is a melting pot of flavors and cultures, a reflection of who I am. It's a place where I can be both Indian and American, where the aroma of spices reminds me of my roots and the taste of home is just a bite away.

DEDICATION

To Mom, I wanted to take a moment to express my deepest gratitude for our recent trip to India. It was more than just a vacation; it was a journey that deepened my connection to our heritage and to you. Your guidance and support in my quest to master Indian cooking mean more to me than words can express. Each shared recipe is not just a culinary tip but also a piece of our family's history and a bond that ties us together. Thank you for always being my teacher, my guide, and my inspiration. I love you more than words can say.

CHAPTER 1: EXPLORING THE FLAVORS OF INDIA

THE DIVERSITY OF INDIAN CUISINE

India is a land of rich cultural heritage and diverse culinary traditions. Its vast landscape is home to a multitude of regional cuisines, each with its own unique flavors, ingredients, and cooking techniques. Indian cuisine can be broadly categorized into four regions: North, South, East, and West. Each region offers a distinctive culinary experience that reflects its history, geography, and cultural influences.

- ### NORTH INDIAN CUISINE

North Indian cuisine is perhaps the most widely recognized and celebrated outside of India. Known for its rich, creamy gravies and extensive use of dairy products like ghee, butter, and yogurt, it offers a hearty and flavorful dining experience. Key spices include garam masala, coriander, cumin, and cardamom. Staple foods in the north include wheat-based products like naan, roti, and paratha.

Popular dishes from this region include butter chicken, a creamy tomato-based curry; palak paneer, a spinach and cheese delicacy; and chole bhature, a spicy chickpea curry served with deep-fried bread. North Indian cuisine also boasts an array of kebabs and tandoori dishes, which are cooked in a traditional clay oven, imparting a unique smoky flavor. The region's desserts, like gulab jamun and jalebi, are often rich and syrupy—perfect for those with a sweet tooth.

- ### SOUTH INDIAN CUISINE

In stark contrast to the North, South Indian cuisine is characterized by its use of rice, coconut, and tamarind. This region's food is known for its bold and tangy flavors, often tempered with the heat of fresh and dried chilies. Lentils and rice form the base of many dishes, creating a variety of dosas, idlis, and vadas, which are often accompanied by an array of chutneys and sambar, a spicy lentil soup.

Signature dishes from the South include masala dosa, a fermented crepe filled with spicy potato filling; sambar, a lentil-based stew with vegetables; and rasam, a tangy soup seasoned with tamarind and tomatoes. South Indian cuisine also features an extensive range of seafood, thanks to its coastal geography. Dishes like fish curry and prawn masala are beloved for their aromatic spices and flavors. The region's desserts, like payasam and Mysore pak, are typically made with jaggery, coconut, and cardamom, offering a unique and satisfying sweetness.

- ### EAST INDIAN CUISINE

East Indian cuisine, although less known internationally, offers a delightful culinary adventure. This region's cuisine is heavily influenced by its lush, fertile landscape, which produces an abundance of rice, fish, and vegetables. The flavors here are more subtle, often highlighting the natural taste of the ingredients with minimal spice interference.

Bengal, a prominent part of Eastern India, is renowned for its love of fish and sweets. Dishes like macher jhol, a fish curry, and shorshe ilish, hilsa fish cooked in mustard sauce, showcase the region's expertise in seafood. Bengali sweets such as rasgulla, made from chenna (Indian cottage cheese) and soaked in syrup, and sandesh, a delicately flavored milk-based dessert, are famous throughout the country.

In the northeastern states, the cuisine incorporates more fermented foods, bamboo shoots and local herbs, reflecting the influence of neighboring countries like China and Myanmar. Dishes such as momos (dumplings) and thukpa (noodle soup) are popular here, providing a comforting and nourishing meal.

• WEST INDIAN CUISINE

Western India offers a varied culinary landscape that ranges from the spicy and vibrant flavors of Gujarat and Rajasthan to the coastal and coconut-rich cuisine of Goa and Maharashtra. This region's cuisine is a testament to its diverse cultural history and geographic diversity.

Gujarat is known for its vegetarian fare, often featuring a balance of sweet, salty, and spicy flavors. Dishes like dhokla, a fermented rice and chickpea cake, and thepla, a spiced flatbread, are staples. Rajasthani cuisine, on the other hand, is known for its robust and spicy dishes like laal maas, a fiery mutton curry, and dal baati churma, a combination of lentils, baked wheat balls, and sweetened crushed bread.

Goan cuisine reflects its Portuguese colonial past and coastal location, with dishes like vindaloo, a spicy pork curry, and prawn balchão, a tangy shrimp pickle, showcasing the use of vinegar and spices. Maharashtrian cuisine offers a mix of hearty and flavorful dishes like vada pav, a spiced potato fritter in a bun, and puran poli, a sweet flatbread stuffed with lentils and jaggery.

Influences of Geography and Climate on Indian Cuisine

India's diverse geography and varying climate profoundly shape its culinary practices, dictating the ingredients available and the types of dishes prepared. From mountainous regions to coastal areas, each geographical and climatic zone contributes uniquely to the country's rich culinary tapestry.

MOUNTAINOUS AND HILLY REGIONS

The northern and northeastern parts of India, characterized by the Himalayan mountain range and other hilly areas, have a cooler climate. This environment supports crops like wheat, maize, and barley, along with fruits such as apples and cherries. Dairy products are prominent due to livestock farming, leading to dishes rich in ghee and butter, such as parathas and butter chicken. The cold weather also necessitates hearty, warming dishes like Himachal Pradesh's dham, a traditional meal of rice, lentils, and yogurt-based curry.

PLAINS AND FERTILE VALLEYS

The Indo-Gangetic plains, with its fertile soil and moderate climate, is ideal for agriculture. Rice and wheat are staples, influencing dishes such as biryani, pulao, roti and naan. The fertile land supports a variety of vegetables and fruits, resulting in vegetarian dishes like saag and aloo gobi. Spices grow year-round, contributing to the rich flavors of the region's cuisine.

COASTAL REGIONS

India's extensive coastline provides a tropical climate perfect for rice, coconut, and spices like black pepper and curry leaves. The coastal cuisine prominently features seafood, with dishes like fish curry and prawn masala. The abundant coconut palms influence the use of coconut milk, oil, and grated coconut in dishes from Kerala and Goa. Tropical fruits like mangoes and bananas are also widely used.

ARID AND SEMI-ARID REGIONS

Arid regions like Rajasthan and parts of Gujarat rely on drought-resistant crops like millet and legumes due to harsh climatic conditions. The cuisine includes dishes like bajra roti and dal baati churma, with a heavy use of dairy products like buttermilk and ghee. The scarcity of fresh vegetables leads to the use of dried and preserved foods.

RIVERINE AND DELTA REGIONS

The humid, fertile delta regions, including Bengal and Odisha, are ideal for rice cultivation and freshwater fish. Bengali cuisine features fish dishes like macher jhol and shorshe ilish. The humid climate supports a variety of vegetables and fruits, with mustard oil and seeds adding a distinctive flavor to many dishes.

INGREDIENTS AND SPICES

COMMON INGREDIENTS USED IN INDIAN COOKING

Category	Common Ingredients	Uses
Spices	Turmeric, Cumin, Coriander, Garam Masala, Mustard Seeds, Fenugreek	Adds depth, warmth, and complexity to dishes like curries, biryanis, and stews.
Herbs	Cilantro (Coriander Leaves), Mint	Used for garnishing and in chutneys, adding bright and refreshing flavors.
Legumes	Lentils (various types like red, yellow, and black), Chickpeas, Split Peas	Primary protein source in vegetarian dishes, used in soups, stews, and curries.
Grains	Rice (Basmati, regular), Wheat (used for roti, naan, paratha)	Staples in Indian meals, forming the base of many dishes like biryanis, pulaos, and breads.
Vegetables	Tomatoes, Onions, Potatoes, Spinach	Integral to curries, sauces, and a variety of dishes like aloo gobi and palak paneer.
Dairy	Yogurt, Ghee, Paneer	Adds richness and creaminess, used in marinades, curries, and as a side dish.
Nuts and Seeds	Cashews, Almonds, Sesame Seeds	Add texture and flavor, used in gravies, sweets, and snacks.
Fruits	Mangoes (ripe and raw), Coconut (grated, milk, oil)	Adds sweetness and complexity, used in dishes, pickles, chutneys, and desserts.
Oils	Mustard Oil, Coconut Oil	Used for cooking and flavoring, with regional preferences like mustard oil in Eastern/Northern India and coconut oil in South India.

COOKING TECHNIQUES AND UTENSILS

Traditional cooking methods

Indian cuisine is characterized not only by its diverse ingredients but also by its array of traditional cooking methods that have been perfected over centuries. These methods are essential for achieving the authentic flavors and textures that define Indian food. Here are some of the most common traditional cooking methods used in Indian cuisine:

TANDOORI COOKING

Tandoori cooking involves using a tandoor, a cylindrical clay oven heated by charcoal or wood fires. This method is used for cooking bread like naan and roti, as well as marinated meats and vegetables. The high, direct heat from the tandoor creates a distinctive smoky flavor and a charred exterior while keeping the inside tender and juicy. Popular tandoori dishes include tandoori chicken, seekh kebabs, and tandoori paneer.

DUM COOKING

Dum cooking, or slow cooking, is a technique where food is cooked on low heat in a sealed container, usually a heavy-bottomed pot. The lid is often sealed with dough to trap steam and flavor. This method allows the ingredients to cook in their own juices, intensifying the flavors. Dum biryani, where rice and meat or vegetables are cooked together with spices, is a classic example of this technique. Dum aloo, a potato curry, also utilizes this method.

BHUNA

Bhuna refers to a method of cooking in which spices and ingredients are fried in oil or ghee, over medium to high heat, allowing the flavors to develop and intensify. This method is often used at the beginning of making a curry, where onions, garlic, ginger, and spices are cooked until they release their essential oils and become aromatic. The term "bhuna" can also refer to a dish prepared using this technique, such as bhuna gosht (spicy fried meat).

TADKA

Tadka, also known as tempering, involves frying whole spices in hot oil or ghee to release their essential oils and enhance their flavors before adding them to a dish. This method is commonly used in Indian dals (lentil soups) and curries. The hot oil or ghee is poured over the cooked dish at the end, adding a burst of flavor. Common spices used in tadka includes mustard seeds, cumin seeds, curry leaves, and dried red chilies.

GRILLING AND ROASTING

Grilling and roasting are widely used in Indian cooking, particularly for meats and vegetables. Skewers of marinated meat, fish, or paneer are grilled over an open flame or roasted in an oven. This method imparts a smoky flavor and charred texture. Popular dishes include kebabs, tikkas, and roasted vegetables like baingan bharta (roasted eggplant mash).

STEAMING

Steaming is a healthier cooking method often used in South Indian cuisine. Idli (steamed rice cakes) and dhokla (steamed fermented chickpea flour cakes) are famous examples. This method preserves nutrients and natural flavors, making it ideal for breakfast and snacks.

PRESSURE COOKING

Pressure cooking is a method that uses steam pressure to cook food quickly. This technique is commonly used in Indian kitchens to prepare lentils, beans, and rice dishes. The pressure cooker reduces cooking time while retaining the flavors and nutrients of the ingredients. Dishes like dal, rajma (kidney beans), and biryani are often made using this method.

DEEP FRYING

Deep frying is used to prepare a variety of snacks and sweets in Indian cuisine. Ingredients are submerged in hot oil, resulting in a crispy exterior and a soft interior. Popular deep-fried items include samosas (stuffed pastry), pakoras (vegetable fritters), and jalebis (sweet spiral-shaped treats).

BOILING AND SIMMERING

Boiling and simmering are basic yet essential cooking methods used in Indian cuisine. Boiling involves cooking food in water at high temperatures and is often used for rice and vegetables. Simmering, which involves cooking food gently at a lower temperature, is used for making soups, stews, and curries. This method allows flavors to meld and develop over time, resulting in rich and flavorful dishes.

STIR-FRYING

Stir-frying involves cooking ingredients quickly over high heat in a small amount of oil. This method is used to prepare dishes that require minimal cooking time, preserving the crunch and freshness of vegetables. Stir-fried dishes often include a combination of spices, herbs, and sauces, such as vegetable stir-fry or chili paneer.

Essential kitchen tools for Indian recipes

Indian cuisine is known for its diverse flavors, spices, and cooking techniques. To prepare authentic Indian dishes at home, it's helpful to have the right kitchen tools. Here are some essential tools commonly used in Indian cooking:

SPICE GRINDER OR MORTAR AND PESTLE

Whole spices are integral to Indian cooking, and grinding them fresh can elevate the flavor of dishes. A spice grinder or mortar and pestle can be used to grind spices like cumin, coriander, cardamom, and cloves to release their oils and aroma.

PRESSURE COOKER

A pressure cooker is a versatile tool in Indian kitchens, used to cook lentils, beans, and tough cuts of meat quickly. It helps tenderize ingredients and lock in flavors, making it ideal for preparing dishes like dal, rajma, and biryani.

TAVA OR GRIDDLE

A tava is a flat, round griddle used to cook bread like roti, naan, and paratha. It provides a large, flat cooking surface and allows for even cooking, essential for achieving the right texture and taste in Indian breads.

KADAI OR WOK

A kadai is a deep, heavy-bottomed wok used for frying, sautéing, and making curries. It has curved sides that help in stirring and tossing ingredients, making it ideal for preparing dishes like bhindi masala, kadai paneer, and stir-fried vegetables.

ROLLING PIN (BELAN) AND BOARD

A rolling pin and board are used to roll out dough for Indian breads like roti, naan, and puri. The rolling pin, or belan, helps flatten the dough evenly, while the board provides a smooth surface for rolling.

STAINLESS STEEL POTS AND PANS

Stainless steel pots and pans are durable and ideal for cooking Indian dishes. They distribute heat evenly, preventing hot spots and ensuring that food cooks evenly. They are also easy to clean and maintain.

SPICE BOX (MASALA DABBA)

A masala dabba is a traditional Indian spice box with small containers to hold commonly used spices. It helps keep spices organized and easily accessible while cooking, saving time and effort.

BLENDER OR FOOD PROCESSOR

A blender or food processor is essential for making smooth pastes and sauces. It grinds ingredients like onions, tomatoes, and ginger-garlic into a fine paste, which forms the base of many Indian curries and gravies.

CHOPPING BOARD AND SHARP KNIFE

A good chopping board and sharp knife are essential for cutting and chopping vegetables, fruits, and meats. They help in preparing ingredients quickly and efficiently, which is important in Indian cooking, where many dishes require finely chopped ingredients.

SIEVE OR STRAINER

A sieve or strainer is used to separate solids from liquids or to sift flour and other dry ingredients. It is useful for straining lentils, rice, or tea leaves, and for removing lumps from batter or sauces.

SERVING BOWLS AND PLATES

Indian cuisine often includes multiple dishes served together, so having a variety of serving bowls and plates in different sizes is useful. It allow for presenting and serving dishes in an appealing and organized manner.

COOKING SPOONS AND LADLES

A set of cooking spoons and ladles in different sizes is essential for stirring, mixing, and serving dishes. Wooden or stainless steel spoons are preferred as they do not react with acidic ingredients and are safe to use with hot foods.

TONGS AND SPATULA

Tongs and spatula are useful for flipping and turning food while cooking, especially when using a tava or griddle. They help in handling hot items safely and efficiently.

MEASURING SPOONS AND CUPS

Accurate measurement of ingredients is crucial in Indian cooking, especially when using spices and other flavorings. Measuring spoons and cups help ensure consistency and balance in dishes.

In a tantalizing journey through India's culinary landscape, we've uncovered the profound impact of geography and climate on its diverse cuisine. As we venture into the recipes that follow, each dish becomes a gateway to a specific region's flavors, a testament to its unique environment.

From the spicy aromas of the North to the coconut-infused curries of the South, every recipe is a story of tradition and terroir. The tools and techniques we've explored are not just utensils; they're the keys to unlocking centuries-old culinary secrets, ensuring each dish is an authentic expression of its heritage.

This culinary adventure, let the influence of geography and climate guide your journey through the tantalizing flavors of India. Explore, experiment, and savor the essence of a culture deeply connected to its land.

CHAPTER 2: SPICE BLENDS, CHUTNEYS AND RELISHES

STEAMED TEMPEH

Prep time: 10 minutes | Cook time: 10 minutes | Makes 2 ¼ cup

- 8 ounces tempeh, cut into ½-inch cubes
- 1 cup water
- ¼ teaspoon salt
- ¼ teaspoon garam masala
- ¼ teaspoon garlic powder
- ¼ teaspoon ground ginger
- ¼ teaspoon smoked paprika (or hot paprika for more heat)

1. Combine all ingredients in a medium skillet or saucepan.
2. Bring to a simmer over medium heat and cook for 10-12 minutes, or until most of the water is absorbed.
3. Remove from heat and let stand for 5 minutes.
4. Drain any excess liquid before serving.

HOMEMADE SAMBAR POWDER

Prep time: 10 minutes | Cook time: 10 minutes | Makes 2 cups

- 1 teaspoon black mustard seeds
- 1 teaspoon fenugreek seeds
- 2 teaspoons cumin seeds
- 1 teaspoon black peppercorns
- 1 teaspoon coriander seeds
- 1 teaspoon toor dal (split pigeon peas)
- 1 teaspoon urad dal (split black lentils)
- 1 teaspoon ground turmeric
- ¼ teaspoon asafoetida (hing)

1. Heat a heavy-bottomed skillet over medium-low heat. Working with one spice at a time, dry-toast each whole spice, stirring constantly until fragrant and lightly darkened, about 1-2 minutes each. Transfer to a bowl as done.
2. In the same pan, dry-toast the toor dal for 5-6 minutes until golden brown. Add to the spice mixture.
3. Dry-toast the urad dal for 4-5 minutes until lightly golden. Add to the spice mixture.
4. Allow the mixture to cool completely.
5. Add the turmeric and asafoetida to the cooled spices.
6. Grind everything to a fine powder using a spice grinder or mortar and pestle.

TRADITIONAL GARAM MASALA

Prep time: **15 minutes** | **Cook time:** **10 minutes** | **Makes** **1½ cups**

- ½ cup coriander seeds
- ¼ cup cumin seeds
- 6-8 cinnamon sticks (2-inch pieces)
- 8-10 black cardamom pods
- 2 tablespoons green cardamom pods
- 2 tablespoons whole cloves
- 1-1½ tablespoons black peppercorns
- 10-12 Indian bay leaves (tej patta)
- 1 whole nutmeg (optional)

1. If storing whole: Combine all ingredients and store in an airtight container for up to 1 year.

To make ground garam masala:

2. First grind the cinnamon sticks and nutmeg (if using) in a spice grinder until finely ground
3. Add remaining spices and grind to a fine powder
4. Store in an airtight container for up to 3 months

BASIC TOMATO MASALA

Prep time: **10 minutes** | **Cook time:** **30 minutes** | **Makes** **Enough for one curry (Serves 4)**

- 2 tablespoons canola or vegetable oil
- 1 medium onion, finely chopped
- 1¼-inch piece fresh ginger, peeled and minced
- 2-3 garlic cloves, minced
- 1 fresh green or red chili, finely chopped (or ½ teaspoon red chili powder)
- 1 (14.5 oz) can diced tomatoes, drained and divided
- 1 tablespoon tomato paste

1. Heat oil in a large skillet or sauté pan over medium heat. Add onion and cook for 6-8 minutes, stirring occasionally, until soft and golden brown.
2. Add ginger, garlic, and chili. Cook for 3-4 minutes, stirring frequently.
3. Add tomatoes and tomato paste. Reduce heat to low, cover, and simmer for 8-10 minutes, stirring occasionally, until the sauce thickens and deepens in color.
4. Let cool completely before storing.

SPICY GARLIC-COCONUT CHUTNEY

Prep time: 15 minutes | **Cook time:** 15 minutes | **Makes** 1½ cups

- 1 teaspoon coconut oil or safflower oil
- 3 tablespoons garlic paste (or 7 cloves garlic, minced)
- 1½ teaspoons cayenne pepper (or 1 teaspoon cayenne + ½ teaspoon paprika for milder heat)
- 1 cup water, divided
- ½ cup unsweetened shredded coconut (dried or fresh)
- 2 tablespoons sesame seeds
- ½ teaspoon salt

Tempering (Tadka)

- 1 teaspoon coconut oil or safflower oil
- ½ teaspoon black mustard seeds
- ¼ teaspoon cumin seeds
- Pinch of asafetida (hing)
- 6-8 curry leaves, roughly chopped

1. In a medium skillet over medium heat, warm oil. Add garlic and cook until golden and fragrant, about 2 minutes.
2. Stir in cayenne pepper briefly, then add ¼ cup water. Mix in coconut and sesame seeds.
3. Remove from heat and let cool for 10 minutes.
4. Transfer mixture to a blender. Add remaining ¾ cup water and salt. Pulse until well combined but not overly smooth.
5. For the tempering: Heat oil in a small skillet over medium heat. Add mustard seeds and cumin seeds; cook until they begin to pop (about 30 seconds).
6. Add asafetida and curry leaves; cook until leaves become crisp, about 30 seconds.
7. Pour tempering over chutney and gently stir to combine.

HOMEMADE MASALA CHAI SPICE BLEND

Prep time: 10 minutes | **Cook time:** 10 minutes | **Makes** about ½ cup

- 4 tablespoons ground ginger
- 2 tablespoons ground cinnamon
- 2 tablespoons ground cloves
- 1 tablespoon ground black pepper
- 1 tablespoon ground cardamom

1. Put the spices in a jar, screwing the lid on very tightly before shaking vigorously to mix them.
2. Keep in a cool, dark place for up to 6 months.

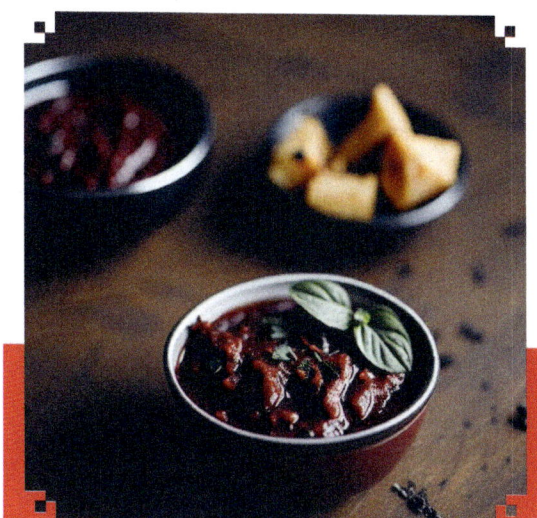

FRESH CILANTRO-PEANUT CHUTNEY

Prep time: 10 minutes | **Cook time:** 10 minutes | **Makes** ¾ cup (6 oz)

- 2 bunches fresh cilantro (about 4 cups packed)
- ½ cup raw unsalted peanuts
- ¼ cup fresh lemon juice (about 2 lemons)
- 1 teaspoon kosher salt
- 4 teaspoons light brown sugar
- ¼ teaspoon ground turmeric
- 2-3 serrano peppers, roughly chopped (remove seeds for less heat)
- 2-3 tablespoons water, as needed

1. Clean cilantro by submerging in a bowl of cold water. Swish gently, lift out, and shake off excess water. Pat dry with paper towels.
2. Roughly chop cilantro (stems and leaves) and add to a food processor. Add peanuts, lemon juice, salt, brown sugar, turmeric, and 2 serrano peppers.
3. Pulse until smooth, adding water 1 tablespoon at a time to achieve a pesto-like consistency.
4. Taste and adjust seasoning with additional chile, lemon juice, salt, or sugar as needed.

TOMATO AND GINGER CHUTNEY

Prep time: 10 minutes | **Cook time:** 20 minutes | **Makes** 1 cup (**Serves** 4)

- 2 large tomatoes (about 12 ounces), peeled, seeded, and finely chopped
- 2 teaspoons fresh ginger, peeled and finely grated
- 2 cloves garlic, minced
- ¼ teaspoon kosher salt
- ¼ teaspoon Indian red chile powder (or cayenne)
- 2 tablespoons neutral oil (such as canola or peanut)
- ¼ teaspoon urad dal (split black lentils, available at Indian grocery stores)
- ¼ teaspoon whole mustard seeds
- 5-6 fresh curry leaves, lightly crushed

1. In a medium bowl, combine tomatoes, ginger, garlic, salt, and chile powder.
2. Heat oil in a small nonstick skillet over medium-high heat. Add urad dal and cook until it begins to turn golden, about 30 seconds.
3. Add mustard seeds. When they begin to pop (a few seconds), quickly add curry leaves (they will splutter), followed immediately by the tomato mixture.
4. Cook, stirring constantly, until mixture thickens into a dark paste, 7-8 minutes.
5. Let cool, then remove curry leaves before serving.

13

HONEY-MUSTARD TADKA RAITA

Prep time: 5 minutes | Cook time: 5 minutes | Makes 1 cup

- ¾ cup plain whole-milk yogurt, at room temperature
- 3 tablespoons fresh cilantro, finely chopped
- 1 tablespoon honey
- 2 tablespoons fresh lime juice (about 1 lime)
- 2 tablespoons neutral oil (such as canola)
- 1 tablespoon black or brown mustard seeds
- 10 fresh curry leaves (optional)
- ½ teaspoon ground turmeric
- 1 tablespoon ginger-garlic paste (or 2 cloves minced garlic + 1 tablespoon minced fresh ginger)
- Kosher salt to taste

1. In a medium bowl, whisk together yogurt, cilantro, honey, and lime juice until smooth and creamy. Let stand at room temperature while preparing the tadka (tempering).
2. For the tadka: Heat oil in a small skillet over medium-high heat. Add mustard seeds and cook until they begin to pop, about 30 seconds.
3. Reduce heat to medium-low. Add curry leaves (they will splutter), turmeric, and ginger-garlic paste. Stir continuously for 30 seconds until fragrant.
4. Immediately pour the hot seasoned oil mixture over the yogurt. Whisk quickly to incorporate and prevent the yogurt from curdling.
5. Season with salt to taste. Refrigerate for 1 hour before serving to allow flavors to develop.
6. Serve chilled as a cooling accompaniment to spicy curries, biryani, or grilled meats. Keeps refrigerated for up to 2 days.

CHAPTER 3: RICE AND FLOURS

SPICED EGGPLANT BIRYANI-STYLE RICE

Prep time: 10 minutes | **Cook time:** 30 minutes | **Serves** 4

- 2 tablespoons vegetable oil
- 1 medium yellow onion, thinly sliced
- ⅛ teaspoon asafoetida (hing) powder (optional)
- 8-10 fresh curry leaves (or 15 dried)
- 1 medium eggplant (about 1 pound), cut into 1-inch cubes
- 10 whole cashews
- 1 teaspoon ground turmeric
- 1 teaspoon Indian red chile powder or cayenne (adjust to taste)
- 1 tablespoon goda masala (see note)
- 1 cup basmati rice, rinsed until water runs clear
- 2 teaspoons fresh lemon juice
- ½ teaspoon kosher salt, or to taste
- 2 cups water
- For serving (optional): Plain yogurt, mango pickle, and poppadoms

1. Heat oil in a large heavy-bottomed pot over medium-high heat. Add onion and curry leaves, cooking until onion begins to brown, 5-7 minutes.
2. Add asafoetida (if using), eggplant, and cashews. Cook until eggplant begins to soften, about 5 minutes.
3. Stir in turmeric, chile powder, and goda masala. Cook for 1 minute until fragrant.
4. Add rice and stir to coat with spices. Add water, lemon juice, and salt. Bring to a boil.
5. Reduce heat to low, cover, and cook for 15 minutes or until water is absorbed.
6. Let stand covered for 5 minutes, then fluff with a fork.
7. Serve hot with yogurt, pickle, and poppadoms if desired.

BOMBAY SANDWICHES

Prep time: 10 minutes | **Cook time:** 20 minutes | **Serves** 2

- 2 Yukon Gold potatoes (about 8 oz total), boiled until tender and peeled
- 2 medium ripe tomatoes
- ½ large bell pepper (green or red)
- 1 medium yellow onion
- Butter, softened
- 4 large slices white sandwich bread
- Salt and freshly ground black pepper
- About 2 tbsp Mint-Cilantro Chutney
- 2 slices mild cheddar cheese

1. Cut each of the potatoes lengthwise into 5 thin ovals (about ¼-inch thick). Discard the rounded outer pieces. Slice the tomatoes into rounds, discarding the top and bottom slices. Cut off the top and bottom of the bell pepper and remove all seeds. Cut the remaining flesh into thin, long strips. Peel the onion and cut into thin rings.

2. Butter the slices of bread generously. Working with just two slices, arrange potato slices on them in a single layer. Sprinkle lightly with salt and pepper. Layer tomato slices on top of the potatoes and season lightly with salt and pepper. Add the pepper strips and onion rings. Spread the chutney evenly over the vegetables. Place a cheese slice on each sandwich. Top with the remaining buttered bread slices and press down gently.

3. If using a sandwich maker, follow the manufacturer's instructions. Otherwise, heat a heavy, preferably cast-iron skillet over medium heat. When hot, melt about 1 tbsp of butter in the center, then place the two sandwiches in the pan. Press down firmly with a spatula until the bottom is golden brown and the cheese starts to melt, about 3-4 minutes. Carefully flip, add a little more butter if needed, and toast the second side until golden brown.

4. Remove the sandwiches, cut into triangles, and serve hot.

RICE WITH YELLOW SPLIT PEAS

Prep time: 10 minutes | Cook time: 1 hour 20 minutes | Serves 4

- ½ cup yellow split peas (chana dal)
- 4 tsp salt, divided
- 1 cup basmati rice
- 2 tbsp ghee or vegetable oil
- 1 tsp whole cumin seeds
- 2 bay leaves
- 3-4 small pearl onions, peeled and halved
- 3 tbsp butter
- ¼ tsp black pepper
- 2 green cardamom pods, lightly crushed

1. Soak split peas in 2 cups cold water for 1 hour. Drain and rinse.
2. Bring 3 cups water and 1 tsp salt to boil. Add drained split peas, reduce heat, and simmer for 7-8 minutes until tender but still firm. Drain and set aside.
3. Meanwhile, wash rice until water runs clear. In a pot, bring 8 cups water and 2 tsp salt to boil. Add rice, cook for exactly 5 minutes, then drain.
4. Preheat oven to 300°F.
5. In a heavy ovenproof casserole, heat ghee over medium heat. Add cumin seeds and bay leaves; fry 30 seconds until fragrant. Add onions, cook 2 minutes until softened. Add rice, split peas, remaining salt, and pepper. Stir gently for 2 minutes.
6. Dot with butter pieces and add cardamom pods. Cover tightly with foil, then lid. Bake 45 minutes. Let rest 10 minutes before fluffing with fork.

SEMOLINA PANCAKES

Prep time: 10 minutes | Cook time: 25 minutes | Makes 8

- ½ medium onion, finely chopped
- ½ cup coarse semolina (sooji or cream of wheat)
- ¼ tsp ground turmeric
- 1 cup fresh cilantro leaves, finely chopped
- 1-2 serrano chilies, finely diced (adjust to taste)
- 3 tbsp vegetable oil, plus more for cooking
- 1 tsp salt
- ½ tsp cumin seeds (optional)
- ¼ cup grated carrot (optional)

1. Combine the onion, semolina, turmeric, salt, cilantro, and chili in a bowl. Add 1 cup cold water gradually, stirring constantly to make a smooth batter slightly thicker than pancake batter. Add cumin seeds and carrot if using. Let rest for 15-20 minutes - this is essential for the semolina to absorb water and create fluffy pancakes.
2. Heat a large nonstick skillet over medium heat. Add 1 tsp oil. Stir the batter well (it will have thickened), then pour a ladleful (about ¼ cup) into the center and quickly spread it with the back of the ladle into a 5-inch disc. Drizzle ½ tsp oil around the edges, cover with a lid, and cook for 2-3 minutes until the bottom is golden brown with crispy edges.
3. Flip when bubbles appear on the surface and the edges start lifting. Cook the second side uncovered for 1-2 minutes, adding more oil around the edges if needed for crispiness. Transfer to a plate lined with paper towels and cover loosely with foil. Repeat with remaining batter, stirring before each pancake.
4. Serve hot with coconut chutney, mint chutney, or Indian pickle. These pancakes are best eaten immediately while crispy.

RICE WITH DILL AND PEAS

Prep time: 10 minutes | **Cook time: 1 hour 10 minutes** | **Serves 4–6**

- 2 cups aged basmati rice
- 3 tbsp ghee or vegetable oil
- 1 large onion, peeled and sliced into thin half-moons
- 1½ tsp garam masala
- 1 cup fresh dill, finely chopped
- 1 tsp salt
- ¼ tsp black pepper
- 2 green cardamom pods (optional)
- 1½ cups fresh or frozen peas
- 2 tbsp butter (optional, for finishing)

1. Wash rice thoroughly until water runs clear (about 3-4 changes). Soak in cold water for 30 minutes. Drain well in a fine-mesh strainer.
2. Preheat oven to 325°F. Position rack in middle.
3. Heat ghee in a heavy ovenproof Dutch oven over medium-high heat. Add onions and cook for 8-10 minutes, stirring occasionally, until deep golden brown and caramelized. Add garam masala, toast for 30 seconds. Add drained rice, dill, salt, pepper, and cardamom if using. Gently fold together, taking care not to break rice grains. Pour in 2¾ cups hot water (about 180°F), bring to a gentle boil.
4. Cover tightly first with foil (shiny side down), then the lid. Transfer to oven for 20 minutes. Scatter peas over rice (do not stir), re-cover quickly, and cook another 8-10 minutes until rice is tender and peas are heated through.
5. Remove from oven, let rest undisturbed for 15 minutes. Uncover, add butter if using, and fluff gently with a fork. Serve hot.

SAVORY COCONUT PANCAKES

Prep time: 10 minutes | **Cook time: 30 minutes** | **Makes 16 pancakes**

- 1½ cups basmati rice
- ½ cup cooked rice (helps fermentation)
- 1¼ cups thick coconut milk
- ¼ cup warm water
- 2 tsp sugar
- 1 tsp salt
- ½ tsp active dry yeast
- ½ tsp baking soda
- Coconut oil for greasing

1. Rinse rice until water runs clear. Soak in water for 4-5 hours. Drain well. In a high-powered blender, grind soaked rice, cooked rice, and coconut milk until extremely smooth (about 3-4 minutes). The batter should be completely smooth when rubbed between fingers.
2. Transfer to a deep bowl (batter will rise). Mix in sugar and yeast. Cover with plastic wrap and let ferment in a warm place (75-80°F) for 8-12 hours or overnight. The batter should be bubbly and slightly sour.
3. Just before cooking, stir in salt and baking soda. The batter should be the consistency of thick cream - add warm water if needed.
4. Heat an appam pan or small wok over medium-high heat. Brush lightly with coconut oil. When hot (water droplets should sizzle), pour about ⅓ cup batter in the center. Immediately pick up pan and swirl to spread batter up the sides, creating a thin edge and thicker center.
5. Cover and cook for 1-2 minutes until edges are lacy and crisp, center is cooked but still soft. Edges should be golden brown. Serve immediately with curry or stew.

SWEET PILAF

Prep time: 10 minutes | **Cook time:** 55 minutes | **Serves** 4–6

- 2 cups aged basmati rice
- 3 tbsp ghee or vegetable oil
- 4 whole cloves
- 5 green cardamom pods, lightly crushed
- 4 black peppercorns
- 2 bay leaves
- 1 cinnamon stick
- 1 large onion, thinly sliced
- 2 tbsp ground coriander
- ½ tsp ground cinnamon
- ¼ tsp freshly grated nutmeg
- 3 cups rich beef or lamb stock
- 1 tsp salt (adjust if using salted stock)
- 2 tbsp brown sugar or jaggery
- ¼ cup golden raisins (optional)
- ¼ cup sliced almonds, toasted (optional)

1. Wash rice until water runs clear. Soak in cold water for 30 minutes. Drain well.
2. In a heavy-bottomed Dutch oven, heat ghee over medium heat. Add whole spices (cloves, cardamom, peppercorns, bay leaves, cinnamon stick). Fry 30 seconds until fragrant. Add onions, cook 7-8 minutes until deep golden brown.
3. Add drained rice, ground spices. Stir gently for 2-3 minutes until rice is coated and toasted. Add hot stock and salt. Bring to boil, reduce heat to lowest setting, cover tightly. Cook 15 minutes.
4. Sprinkle sugar and raisins (if using) over rice. Do not stir. Cover, cook 10-15 minutes until rice is tender. Let rest 10 minutes undisturbed.
5. Fluff with fork, top with almonds if using. Serve hot.

CHAPTER 4:
MEAT

SPICED MEATBALL CURRY

Prep time: 10 minutes | Cook time: 40 minutes | Serves 4

For the meatballs:
- 2 cups ground lamb (80/20 fat ratio)
- 3 tbsp ginger-garlic paste
- 2-3 green chilies, finely minced
- 1 tsp garam masala
- 1 egg (helps binding)
- ¼ cup breadcrumbs
- Salt to taste

For the curry sauce:
- 3 tbsp ghee or oil
- 2 bay leaves
- 2 black cardamom pods
- 3 large onions, finely chopped
- 2 tbsp ginger-garlic paste
- 2-3 green chilies, slit
- 3 ripe tomatoes, pureed
- 1 tsp turmeric
- 2 tsp coriander powder
- 1 tsp cumin powder
- 1½ tsp garam masala
- Salt to taste
- Water as needed

1. Mix all meatball ingredients thoroughly. Shape into 20 golf ball-sized koftas. Preheat oven to 400°F. Bake meatballs 12-15 minutes until browned.
2. Meanwhile, heat ghee in heavy pot. Add whole spices, fry 30 seconds. Add onions, cook until deep golden (10-12 minutes). Add ginger-garlic paste, chilies, cook 2 minutes.
3. Add tomato puree, ground spices, salt. Cook 10-12 minutes until oil separates. Add 1 cup water if needed.
4. Gently add meatballs, simmer 8-10 minutes until sauce thickens. Adjust seasoning.
5. Garnish with cilantro, serve hot with rice or naan.

LAMB MASALA CURRY

Prep time: 20 minutes | Cook time: 1 hour | Serves 8

- 3 lb lamb shoulder, cut into 1½-inch pieces
- ¾ cup ghee or oil
- 3 bay leaves
- 2-inch cinnamon stick
- 4 black cardamom pods
- 2 tbsp cumin seeds
- 2 tbsp coriander seeds
- 2 star anise
- 3 large onions, finely sliced
- 5 tbsp ginger-garlic paste
- 4 ripe tomatoes, pureed
- 2 tsp ground turmeric
- 2 tbsp meat masala (or garam masala)
- 1½ tbsp Kashmiri chili powder
- 1 cup full-fat yogurt, whisked
- Salt to taste
- Whole spices for finishing (optional):
- 4 green cardamom pods
- 2 bay leaves
- 1-inch cinnamon

1. Heat ghee in heavy-bottomed pot. Add whole spices, fry 1 minute until fragrant. Add onions, cook 12-15 minutes until deep golden brown.
2. Add ginger-garlic paste, cook 2 minutes. Add tomato puree, cook until oil separates (8-10 minutes).
3. Add turmeric, masalas, chili powder. Cook 2 minutes. Add lamb, brown well (5-7 minutes).
4. Add 2 cups hot water, bring to boil. Reduce heat, simmer covered 45-60 minutes until meat is tender.
5. Add whisked yogurt gradually. Simmer 5 minutes. Add finishing whole spices if using.
6. Garnish with cilantro. Serve with naan or rice.

LAMB STEW

Prep time: 10 minutes | **Cook time: 1 hour** | **Serves 4**

- 3 tbsp ghee or neutral oil
- 3-inch cinnamon stick
- 3 Indian bay leaves
- 25 black peppercorns
- 6 green cardamom pods
- 2 black cardamom pods
- 1½ pounds lamb shoulder, cut into 1½-inch cubes
- 2 large onions, cut into 8 wedges each
- 3 carrots, cut diagonally into 2-inch chunks
- 3 Yukon Gold potatoes, cut into 2-inch cubes
- 4 Kashmiri dried red chiles, broken
- 2 tbsp ginger-garlic paste
- 1½ tbsp kosher salt
- 1½ tsp Kashmiri red chile powder
- 1 cup water or stock
- ½ cup chopped fresh cilantro
- 2 tbsp garam masala

1. Select high Sauté on Instant Pot, heat ghee. Add whole spices, sauté 1-2 minutes until fragrant. Add lamb in batches, sear until golden brown (3-4 minutes per batch). Remove lamb.
2. In same pot, add onions, sauté 3-4 minutes until edges brown. Add ginger-garlic paste, cook 1 minute. Return lamb, add vegetables, chiles, salt, chile powder, and water. Stir to deglaze pot bottom thoroughly.
3. Seal lid, set Pressure Release to Sealing. Select Meat/Stew, cook 40 minutes at high pressure. Natural release 15 minutes, then quick release remaining pressure.
4. Open pot, select high Sauté. Simmer 8-10 minutes until sauce thickens. Stir in garam masala.
5. Garnish generously with cilantro. Serve hot with naan or rice.

ROAST LEG OF LAMB

Prep time: 10 minutes | **Cook time: 1 hour 15 minutes** | **Serves 4**

- ½ leg of lamb (about 2.5 lbs)
- 1½ cups full-fat yogurt
- 2 tbsp Kashmiri red chili powder
- 1½ tsp ground turmeric
- 2 tbsp garam masala
- 4 tbsp ginger-garlic paste
- 2 tbsp raw papaya paste (or 1 tsp meat tenderizer)
- 3 tbsp lemon juice
- 3 tbsp mustard oil
- 2 tbsp salt
- 2 onions, thickly sliced
- 4 whole garlic heads, halved
- Fresh mint for garnish

1. Make deep incisions in lamb at 1-inch intervals. Mix all marinade ingredients except onions and garlic. Rub thoroughly into meat, especially into cuts. Refrigerate 8-24 hours.
2. Preheat oven to 350°F. Let lamb come to room temperature (30 minutes).
3. Layer onions and garlic in roasting pan. Place lamb on top, pour in ½ cup water. Cover tightly with foil. Roast 30 minutes per pound for medium (internal temperature 135°F).
4. Remove foil last 20 minutes, brush with pan juices. Broil 5 minutes for crispy exterior.
5. Rest 20 minutes before carving. Serve with reduced pan juices and naan.

KEEMA CURRY

Prep time: 10 minutes | Cook time: 40 minutes | Serves 4

- 4 large garlic cloves
- 2-inch piece fresh ginger
- 3 green Thai chilies (or serrano peppers)
- ¼ cup vegetable oil
- 1 large yellow onion, finely chopped
- 2 tablespoons tomato paste
- 1 teaspoon ground turmeric
- 1 teaspoon Indian red chili powder (or cayenne)
- 2 teaspoons tandoori masala
- 1 teaspoon garam masala
- 1 teaspoon kosher salt
- 2 bay leaves (optional)
- 12 ounces ground lamb
- 2½ cups water
- ¼ cup fresh cilantro, chopped

1. In a food processor, pulse garlic, ginger, and green chilies until finely minced.
2. Heat oil in a large skillet over medium-high heat. Add onion and cook until golden brown, about 8-10 minutes. Add the garlic-ginger paste, tomato paste, and all dry spices (turmeric, chili powder, tandoori masala, garam masala, salt, and bay leaves if using). Cook for 5 minutes, stirring constantly.
3. Add ground lamb and cook for 5 minutes, breaking up any lumps with a wooden spoon.
4. Pour in water, reduce heat to low, cover, and simmer for 30 minutes. Stir occasionally to prevent sticking.
5. Transfer to a serving bowl and garnish with fresh cilantro. Serve hot.

WHOLE SPICED LAMB

Prep time: 10 minutes | Cook time: 1 hour 15 minutes | Serves 4–6

- ½ cup vegetable oil
- 1 (2-inch) cinnamon stick
- 20 whole black peppercorns
- 15 whole cloves
- 10 green cardamom pods
- 2 bay leaves
- 1-2 dried red chilies (adjust to taste)
- 2 pounds boneless lamb shoulder, trimmed and cut into 1-inch cubes
- 1-1½ teaspoons kosher salt, to taste
- 1 teaspoon garam masala (optional)

For Garnish

- 2 tablespoons fresh cilantro, chopped
- ¼ teaspoon freshly ground cardamom seeds

1. Pat the lamb dry thoroughly with paper towels.
2. Heat oil in a heavy-bottomed Dutch oven over medium heat until shimmering. Add spices in sequence: cinnamon stick, peppercorns, cloves, cardamom pods, bay leaves, and dried chilies.
3. When chilies darken slightly (about 30 seconds), add lamb and salt. Stir frequently for 5 minutes until meat begins to sizzle. Reduce heat to low, cover, and simmer for about 1 hour 10 minutes, or until lamb is tender when pierced with a fork.
4. Uncover and cook over medium heat for 3-5 minutes, stirring gently to avoid breaking the meat. The dish is ready when the lamb is brown and tender, with only a coating of spiced oil clinging to the meat.
5. If using, sprinkle with garam masala before serving. Garnish with cilantro and ground cardamom.

SINDHI-STYLE MARINATED LAMB

Prep time: 10 minutes | Cook time: 1 hour | Serves 6

For the Marinade

- 2 medium yellow onions, roughly chopped
- 2-inch piece fresh ginger
- 6 garlic cloves
- 1 tablespoon ground coriander
- 2 teaspoons ground cumin
- 1 teaspoon ground turmeric
- ⅛-½ teaspoon cayenne pepper (to taste)
- ½ cup red wine vinegar
- 1 teaspoon kosher salt

For the Dish

- 2½ pounds boneless lamb shoulder, cut into 1-inch cubes
- 2 teaspoons fennel seeds
- 1 teaspoon nigella seeds (kalonji)
- ⅓ cup vegetable oil

1. Trim excess fat from lamb cubes.
2. In a blender or food processor, combine all marinade ingredients until smooth.
3. Transfer marinade to a large bowl. Pierce lamb pieces with a fork and add to marinade. Cover and let marinate for 3-4 hours at room temperature (or refrigerate if kitchen is warm).
4. Transfer meat and marinade to a large Dutch oven. Add fennel and nigella seeds. Bring to a boil, then reduce heat, cover, and simmer for about 1 hour or until meat is tender.
5. Uncover and taste for salt. Increase heat to medium-high and cook, stirring frequently, until liquid reduces significantly. Add oil and continue cooking until sauce thickens and clings to the meat, stirring gently to avoid breaking the pieces.

SPICED BEEF CURRY

Prep time: 10 minutes | Cook time: 1 hour 20 minutes | Serves 4

- 1 pound beef chuck or stewing beef
- 4 large garlic cloves
- 1-inch piece fresh ginger
- 2 green Thai chilies (or serrano peppers)
- 2 plum tomatoes, peeled
- ¼ cup vegetable oil
- 1 large yellow onion, finely chopped
- ½ teaspoon ground turmeric
- 2 tablespoons tomato paste
- ½ teaspoon Indian red chili powder (or cayenne)
- 1 teaspoon garam masala
- 1 teaspoon kosher salt
- 1 teaspoon tandoori masala
- 4 teaspoons soy sauce
- 3 cups water
- ¼ cup fresh cilantro, chopped

1. Cut beef into 1-inch cubes, trimming excess fat.
2. In a food processor, blend garlic, ginger, chilies, and tomatoes into a smooth paste.
3. Heat oil in a large Dutch oven over medium-high heat. Add onion and cook until golden brown, about 8-10 minutes. Add beef, spice paste, and all dry spices (turmeric, tomato paste, chili powder, garam masala, salt, tandoori masala) and soy sauce. Cook for 2 minutes, stirring constantly.
4. Reduce heat to low, cover, and simmer for 20 minutes, stirring occasionally. Add water, bring to a simmer, and cook for 1 hour or until beef is tender.
5. Transfer to a serving bowl and garnish with fresh cilantro.

CHAPTER 5: CHICKEN AND EGGS

CREAMY CHICKEN CURRY

Prep time: 10 minutes | **Cook time:** 40 minutes | **Serves** 4

- 1 large onion, thinly sliced
- 1 fresh green chili, chopped
- ¼ cup unsalted cashews
- 3 tablespoons vegetable oil
- 2 teaspoons ginger-garlic paste
- 4 cups skinless, cubed chicken breast
- 1 teaspoon ground coriander
- 1 teaspoon ground cumin
- ½ teaspoon garam masala, plus extra for garnish
- ½ teaspoon ground turmeric
- 2 tablespoons heavy cream (optional)
- Salt, to taste
- Boiled rice, naan, or parathas, for serving

1. Combine the onion, chili, and cashews in a saucepan with a small amount of water. Bring to a boil, then simmer for 10 minutes, or until the onion is soft. Blend into a smooth paste, adding water as needed, and set aside.
2. Heat the oil in a heavy-bottomed saucepan over medium-high heat. Add the ginger-garlic paste, followed by the chicken. Sauté until the chicken is lightly browned and sealed.
3. Stir in the spices (coriander, cumin, garam masala, and turmeric) and salt. Add the onion-cashew paste and a few tablespoons of water from the blender to deglaze the pan. Cook for 12–15 minutes, stirring occasionally, until the chicken is fully cooked.
4. Stir in the heavy cream (if using), and heat through. Taste and adjust seasoning as needed. Garnish with a sprinkle of garam masala and serve hot with rice or bread.

TAWA CHICKEN WING FRY

Prep time: 5 minutes | **Cook time:** 10 minutes | **Serves** 4

- 3 tablespoons canola oil or rendered chicken fat
- 2.2 pounds skinless chicken wings, whole or halved
- 1 teaspoon salt, or to taste
- 2 tablespoons garlic-ginger paste
- 1 teaspoon ground turmeric
- 1 tablespoon ground coriander
- 1 tablespoon tandoori masala
- 1 teaspoon Kashmiri chili powder (adjust to taste)
- ¾ cup water or chicken stock
- 1 large tomato, diced
- 1 handful fresh cilantro, chopped
- 15 fresh or frozen curry leaves
- Juice of 1 lemon

1. Heat the oil in a large skillet over medium-high heat. Add the chicken wings and stir to coat. Sprinkle with salt and add the garlic-ginger paste, stirring to combine.
2. Add the turmeric, coriander, tandoori masala, and chili powder. Stir well to coat the wings evenly. Pour in the water or chicken stock and stir in the diced tomato. Add half of the cilantro and the curry leaves.
3. Continue stirring until the liquid reduces to a thick gravy and the chicken is cooked through. Ensure the wings are moist but not overly saucy.
4. Squeeze fresh lemon juice over the chicken and garnish with the remaining cilantro. Adjust seasoning as needed and serve immediately.

WHOLE ROAST MASALA CHICKEN

Prep time: 10 minutes | **Cook time:** 1 hour 30 minutes | **Serves** 4

- 1 tablespoon cumin seeds
- ¾ tablespoon coriander seeds
- 2-inch cinnamon stick
- 5 cloves
- 1 teaspoon black peppercorns
- ¼ cup ground almonds
- ¼ teaspoon ground turmeric
- 4 tablespoons whole-milk yogurt
- 1¾ teaspoons salt
- ¼ medium onion, roughly chopped
- 3 garlic cloves, roughly chopped
- 1 whole chicken (about 3½ pounds)

1. Toast the cumin and coriander seeds in a dry skillet over high heat until aromatic and lightly golden. Transfer to a spice grinder along with the cinnamon, cloves, and peppercorns. Grind into a fine powder.
2. In a large bowl, mix the spice blend with the ground almonds, turmeric, yogurt, and salt. Mash the onion and garlic into a paste with a pinch of salt and stir into the marinade.
3. Prepare a baking dish lined with foil. Make small slits in the chicken near the thighs and breasts. Rub the marinade under the skin and over the entire chicken. Cover and refrigerate for at least 1 hour or up to 12 hours.
4. Preheat the oven to 400°F. Place the chicken in the baking dish, loosely covering it with foil to prevent burning. Roast for 1 hour, then remove the foil and roast for an additional 20 minutes to brown. Check doneness by piercing the thigh; the juices should run clear.
5. Serve hot with roasted potatoes and spinach sautéed with garlic, black pepper, and lemon.

SPICY SCRAMBLED EGGS

Prep time: 10 minutes | **Cook time:** 10 minutes | **Serves** 4

- 6 large free-range eggs
- 1 tbsp vegetable oil
- 1 large onion, finely chopped
- 1 tsp ginger-garlic paste
- 1–2 fresh green chillies, finely chopped (adjust to taste)
- 2 tomatoes, finely chopped
- A handful of fresh coriander leaves, finely chopped
- Salt and freshly ground black pepper
- Bread, to serve

1. In a bowl, beat the eggs until fluffy. Season with salt and black pepper.
2. Heat oil in a frying pan over high heat. Add the onion and sauté for 5–6 minutes until softened. Stir in the ginger-garlic paste, chillies, and tomatoes. Cook until the mixture is well blended.
3. Reduce heat to medium. Add the eggs and coriander, stirring gently as the eggs cook, about 3 minutes. Adjust cooking time to your preferred texture.
4. Season to taste and serve immediately with fresh bread.

CILANTRO CHUTNEY CHICKEN

Prep time: 10 minutes | **Cook time:** 45 minutes | **Serves** 4

- 2-inch piece of ginger, peeled and roughly chopped
- 6 cloves garlic, roughly chopped
- ¾ fresh green chili, roughly chopped (seeded for less heat)
- Salt, to taste
- 2 tbsp canola oil
- 2 onions, finely sliced
- 1¾ lbs skinless, boneless chicken thighs, cut into ¾-inch pieces
- 6 tbsp cilantro chutney

1. Using a mortar and pestle, pound the ginger, garlic, chili, and a pinch of salt into a coarse paste.
2. Heat oil in a wide, lidded frying pan over medium heat. Add the onions and sauté for 6–8 minutes until golden. Transfer half the onions to a bowl and set aside.
3. Stir in the ginger-garlic paste and cook for 3 minutes. Add the chicken, searing on all sides. Stir in the chutney, cover with a lid, and cook on medium-low heat for 15 minutes until the chicken is tender.
4. Meanwhile, in a separate pan, cook the reserved onions over medium heat for 10–15 minutes until caramelized.
5. Season the chicken with salt, adjusting to taste, and remove from heat. Garnish with caramelized onions and serve with basmati rice or chapatis.

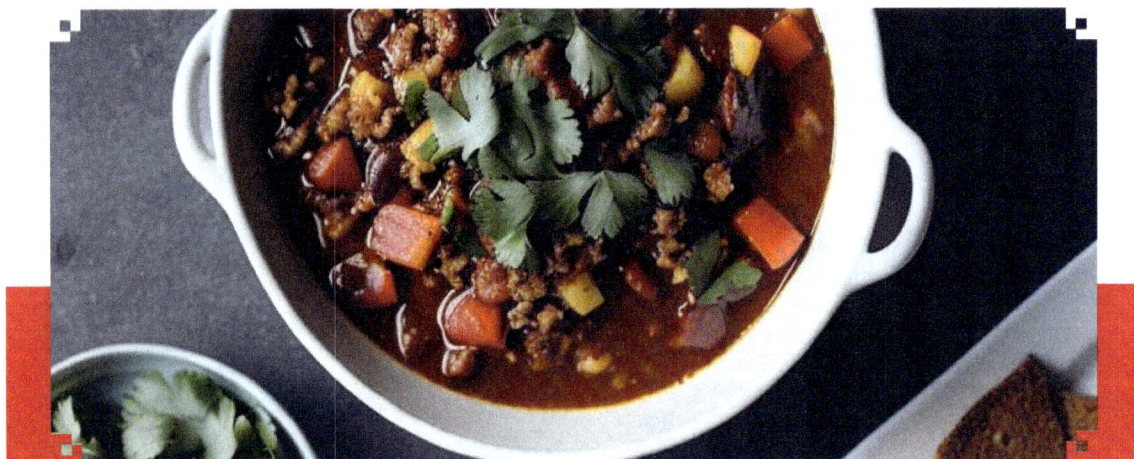

FRESH INDIAN CHEESE COOKED LIKE SCRAMBLED EGGS

Prep time: 10 minutes | Cook time: 10 minutes | Serves 2

- 1 tbsp olive oil or peanut oil
- 5 tbsp finely chopped onion (about ½ medium onion)
- Generous pinch of ground turmeric
- 1 fresh green chili, finely chopped (adjust to taste)
- 1 tsp freshly grated ginger
- 4 medium cherry tomatoes, each cut into eighths
- 7 oz fresh Indian cheese (paneer), crumbled into small pieces
- 3 tbsp cooked green peas (fresh or thawed frozen peas)
- ½ tsp salt (or to taste)
- Freshly ground black pepper
- 2 tbsp chopped fresh cilantro

1. Heat the oil in a medium nonstick skillet over medium heat. Once hot, add the onions and sauté for 1 minute. Stir in the turmeric and green chili, cooking for another 2–3 minutes until the onions soften.
2. Add the ginger and cook for a few seconds, then mix in the tomatoes and stir for 1 minute.
3. Add the crumbled paneer, peas, and salt. Cook on medium-low heat, stirring gently for 2–3 minutes until everything is heated through and evenly mixed.
4. Sprinkle with black pepper and cilantro. Stir again and adjust seasoning to taste before serving.

SPICY GROUND CHICKEN CHILI

Prep time: 10 minutes | Cook time: 30 minutes | Serves 4

- 2 tbsp vegetable oil
- 1 tsp cumin seeds
- 1 large yellow onion, finely diced
- 1 lb ground chicken
- 1 tbsp grated fresh ginger
- 1 tbsp minced garlic
- 2 tsp Kashmiri red chile powder (or mild substitute)
- 1½ tsp kosher salt
- ½ tsp ground turmeric
- 2 plum tomatoes, finely diced (or 1 cup canned puree)
- 1 yellow potato, peeled and diced into ½-inch cubes
- ¼ cup water
- 2 tbsp ground coriander
- 1 tsp garam masala
- ½ cup chopped fresh cilantro

1. Select the Sauté setting on an Instant Pot and heat the oil. Add cumin seeds and fry until aromatic, about 1 minute. Add onion and sauté until soft, about 4–5 minutes.
2. Add chicken, ginger, garlic, chile powder, salt, and turmeric. Cook, breaking up the meat with a spoon. Cancel the Sauté function.
3. Add tomatoes, potatoes, and water, stirring to combine. Sprinkle coriander and garam masala on top without stirring.
4. Secure the lid and set the Pressure Release to Sealing. Pressure cook on high for 4 minutes.
5. Allow pressure to release naturally for 10 minutes, then manually release any remaining steam. Open the pot and sprinkle with cilantro.

CHICKEN AND SPINACH CURRY

Prep time: 10 minutes | **Cook time:** 45 minutes | **Serves** 4

- 1 bunch fresh spinach, washed
- 2 tbsp chopped fresh dill
- ¼ cup chopped fresh cilantro
- 2 tbsp + 1 tsp vegetable oil
- 2 medium onions, thinly sliced
- 1 tsp dried fenugreek leaves (optional)
- 2 fresh green chilies, finely chopped
- 2 tbsp ginger-garlic paste
- 2 tbsp tomato paste
- 1.8 lbs chicken drumsticks, skinned and
- halved at the joint
- 1 tsp ground turmeric
- 1 tsp medium chili powder
- 1 tsp ground coriander
- 1 tsp garam masala
- 1 tbsp lemon juice
- 2 whole green chilies, slit lengthwise (optional, for garnish)
- Salt (to taste)
- Rotis, parathas, or steamed rice (for serving)

1. Place the spinach in a medium saucepan over medium heat. Cook for 3–4 minutes until wilted. Remove from the heat, and transfer the spinach, dill, and cilantro to a blender with a few tablespoons of water. Blend into a smooth purée and set aside.
2. Heat 2 tbsp of the oil in a heavy-bottomed pan over medium-high heat. Add the onions and sauté for 7–8 minutes until softened and lightly golden.
3. Stir in the fenugreek leaves (if using), chopped chilies, ginger-garlic paste, and tomato paste. Cook for 2–3 minutes, adding a splash of water if needed to prevent sticking.
4. Add the chicken, and cook for 2–3 minutes to lightly brown. Stir in the turmeric, chili powder, coriander, garam masala, and salt. Drizzle in the lemon juice and mix well. Add ¾ cup water, bring to a boil, then reduce heat, cover, and simmer for 20–25 minutes, stirring occasionally, until the chicken is tender.
5. Stir in the puréed spinach mixture and cook for another 3–5 minutes. Adjust the seasoning and remove from heat.
6. For an optional garnish, heat 1 tsp of oil in a small skillet. Fry the slit green chilies for 40–60 seconds until slightly blistered, then spoon them and their oil over the curry. Serve hot with rotis, parathas, or steamed rice.

CHAPTER 6: FISH AND SEAFOOD

TANDOORI WHOLE FISH

Prep time: 10 minutes | **Cook time:** 15 minutes | **Serves** 2

- 2 whole bream or sea bass, cleaned
- 1 lemon, quartered

For the Marinade:

- 1 tbsp garlic-ginger paste
- 4 tbsp white wine vinegar
- 1 tsp canola oil
- 1 tsp chili powder
- 2 tbsp tandoori masala
- 1 tsp garam masala
- 1½ tbsp plain yogurt
- Salt, to taste

1. Make shallow slits on both sides of the fish. Combine all marinade ingredients (up to and including the yogurt) in a bowl and whisk until smooth. Season with salt, then rub the marinade all over the fish, inside and out. Let marinate for 30 minutes.
2. Preheat a grill for direct cooking. Remove the fish from the marinade and place it in a metal grill basket, or thread a few skewers through to hold it steady. Grill the fish, turning regularly, until the skin is charred and the flesh is fully cooked. Serve with lemon wedges.

SHRIMP WITH CRUSHED MUSTARD SEEDS

Prep time: 10 minutes | **Cook time:** 10 minutes | **Serves** 4

- 1 lb shrimp, peeled and deveined
- 1 tsp black mustard seeds, crushed
- ⅛ tsp ground turmeric
- 2 tbsp tomato sauce
- 4 tbsp olive oil or vegetable oil
- 2 garlic cloves, peeled
- 2 slices fresh ginger (1 inch long, 1 inch wide, and 1/16 inch thick), peeled
- 1 dried red chili pepper
- ¾ tsp salt
- ⅛ tsp freshly ground black pepper
- 1 tbsp lemon juice

1. Rinse the shrimp under cold water, pat them dry, and set aside.
2. In a small bowl, mix the crushed mustard seeds, turmeric, tomato sauce, and 2 tbsp water. Set aside.
3. Heat the oil in a 10–12-inch skillet over medium-high heat. Add the garlic, ginger slices, and dried chili pepper. Stir until aromatic, about 30 seconds.
4. Add the shrimp and cook, stirring frequently, until they turn pink and opaque. Stir in the mustard seed paste and reduce the heat to medium-low. Season with salt, black pepper, and lemon juice. Cook for 2 more minutes, then remove from heat and serve immediately.

SWEET AND SOUR FISH CURRY

Prep time: 10 minutes | **Cook time:** 30 minutes | **Serves** 4

- 4 fillets of firm fish (kingfish, tuna, or hake)
- 1 tsp ground turmeric, divided
- 2 tsp minced garlic
- 4 large onions, finely chopped
- 2 fresh green chilies, finely diced
- ¼ cup chopped fresh cilantro
- 3 tbsp vegetable oil
- 2 tbsp tamarind paste, mixed with 2 tbsp water
- Salt, to taste
- Cooked rice, for serving

1. Rub the fish fillets with ½ tsp turmeric, minced garlic, and a pinch of salt.
2. In a bowl, mix the onions, chilies, and cilantro, crushing them with your hands to release their juices.
3. Heat the oil in a large skillet over high heat. Add the fish and cook for 2–3 minutes on each side to sear. Transfer to a plate.
4. Add the onion mixture to the skillet and sauté for 8–9 minutes until soft. Stir in the tamarind paste and remaining turmeric, cooking for 2 minutes.
5. Return the fish to the skillet and cook for 8–9 minutes, turning occasionally, until tender. Adjust seasoning to taste. Serve hot with rice.

COCONUT FISH CURRY

Prep time: 10 minutes | **Cook time:** 25 minutes | **Serves** 4

- 2-inch piece ginger, roughly chopped
- 4 garlic cloves, roughly chopped
- 1 fresh green chili, roughly chopped (seeded for less heat)
- Salt, to taste
- 3 tbsp coconut oil or canola oil
- Optional: 20 fresh curry leaves
- 2 medium onions, thinly sliced
- 2 ripe tomatoes, quartered
- ¾ tsp ground turmeric
- ½ tsp chili powder
- 1¼ cups coconut milk
- 4 skinless fish fillets (5–6½ oz each; e.g., hake, pollock, haddock, or cod)
- 1 lime, quartered

1. Using a mortar and pestle, grind the ginger, garlic, green chili, and a pinch of salt into a paste.
2. Heat the oil in a wide skillet over medium heat. If using curry leaves, fry them for 30 seconds. Add the onions and cook, stirring occasionally, for 8–10 minutes until golden.
3. Stir in the ginger-garlic paste and cook for 2–3 minutes. Add the tomatoes, turmeric, chili powder, and 1½ tsp salt. Cover and simmer for 2 minutes.
4. Dilute the coconut milk with ½ cup water and pour into the skillet. Bring to a gentle boil, then add the fish. Reduce the heat to low, cover, and cook for 5–7 minutes, or until the fish is tender.
5. Serve with a squeeze of lime and steamed rice.

COD FISH CURRY

Prep time: 10 minutes | Cook time: 30 minutes | Serves 4

- ½ oz fresh garlic, peeled
- ½ oz fresh ginger, peeled
- 1 green chilli
- 8 oz plum peeled tomatoes
- 2 oz cooking oil
- 1 large onion, finely chopped
- ½ tsp turmeric powder
- ½ tsp chilli powder
- ½ tsp garam masala
- ½ tsp salt
- 1½ lb cod steaks
- Small handful of fresh coriander (dhaniya), chopped

1. Blend the garlic, ginger, chilli, and tomatoes into a thick paste using a blender or liquidiser.
2. Heat the oil in a large pan over high heat. Add the onion and fry until golden brown.
3. Stir in the blended paste along with the turmeric, chilli powder, garam masala, and salt. Cook for about 2 minutes, then let the mixture simmer for 3 minutes.
4. Place the cod steaks in a large ovenproof dish and spread the spiced mixture evenly over them.
5. Bake in a preheated oven at 350°F for approximately 20 minutes, until the fish is cooked through.
6. Garnish with fresh coriander and serve hot.

CRAB CURRY

Prep time: 10 minutes | Cook time: 15 minutes | Serves 4

- 2 tablespoons sunflower oil
- 1 teaspoon fennel seeds
- 1 teaspoon cumin seeds
- 1 teaspoon black mustard seeds
- 6–8 fresh curry leaves
- 1 medium onion, finely chopped
- 2 garlic cloves, grated
- 1-inch piece of fresh ginger root, peeled and grated
- 1 (14-ounce) can coconut milk
- ½ teaspoon salt
- 1 teaspoon ground turmeric
- 1 teaspoon chili powder
- 1 teaspoon ground coriander
- 4 cups water, if needed
- 14 ounces white crab meat
- ¾ ounce fresh cilantro leaves, finely chopped
- Juice of 1 lemon

1. Heat the oil in a pan over medium heat. Add the fennel, cumin, and mustard seeds, letting them sizzle for a few seconds. Stir in the curry leaves, then add the onion and cook until golden, about 8 minutes. Add the garlic and ginger, cooking for 1 more minute.
2. Stir in the coconut milk, salt, turmeric, chili powder, and ground coriander. Cover and cook on low heat for 5 minutes, allowing the flavors to meld. Add water if the sauce is too thick.
3. Fold in the crab meat and chopped cilantro. Cover and cook on low for another 5 minutes.
4. Stir in the lemon juice. Serve hot.

FISH AND GREEN MANGO CURRY

Prep time: 10 minutes | **Cook time:** 40 minutes | **Serves** 4

- 4 (7-ounce) skinless fillets of firm fish (such as cod, haddock, or bream)
- 1 teaspoon ground turmeric
- 1 tablespoon ginger-garlic paste
- 2 tablespoons vegetable oil
- 2 medium onions, finely diced
- 6–7 fresh or 10 dried curry leaves
- 2 fresh green chilies, diced
- 1 green raw mango, peeled and thickly sliced
- ½ teaspoon medium-hot red chili powder
- 1 teaspoon ground coriander
- 2 cups coconut milk
- Salt, to taste
- Cooked rice, for serving

1. Rub the fish with half the turmeric, half the ginger-garlic paste, and salt. Set aside.
2. Heat the oil in a skillet over high heat. Sauté the onions for 8–10 minutes until very soft. Add the curry leaves, remaining ginger-garlic paste, and chilies, followed by the raw mango. Cook for 2 minutes over medium heat.
3. Stir in the remaining turmeric, chili powder, and ground coriander, cooking for 1 minute. Place the fish in the pan and sear for 2–3 minutes on each side.
4. Add the coconut milk and bring to a near boil. Reduce the heat to medium and simmer for 8–9 minutes, or until the fish is tender. Season with salt. Serve with rice.

PRAWN MASALA CURRY

Prep time: 10 minutes | **Cook time:** 10 minutes | **Serves** 4

- 3 tablespoons canola oil or ghee
- 1 teaspoon mustard seeds
- 1-inch piece of cinnamon stick
- 10 curry leaves (optional)
- 2 tablespoons garlic-ginger paste
- 2 green chilies, finely chopped
- 2 tablespoons curry powder or mixed spice powder
- 3 ½ tablespoons tomato purée
- 1 ¾ cups base curry sauce (warmed)
- 5 ounces raw shrimp, peeled and deveined
- 1 cup thick coconut milk
- 2 tablespoons light soy sauce or coconut aminos
- Small bunch of cilantro, finely chopped
- Salt and freshly ground black pepper, to taste
- Juice of 1–2 limes
- 1 teaspoon garam masala

1. Heat the oil in a large skillet over medium-high heat. Add the mustard seeds and cinnamon stick, cooking until the seeds pop, about 30 seconds. Stir in the curry leaves and fry for 15 seconds until fragrant.
2. Add the garlic-ginger paste and cook until sizzling. Mix in the chilies, curry powder, and tomato purée, followed by ½ cup of the curry sauce. Simmer, stirring occasionally. If the sauce caramelizes on the pan sides, stir it in for added flavor.
3. Add the shrimp and the remaining curry sauce. Simmer until the shrimp are cooked through. Stir in the coconut milk and soy sauce. Mix in the cilantro and season with salt and black pepper.
4. Finish with lime juice and a sprinkle of garam masala. Serve hot.

SEA BASS IN GREEN CHUTNEY

Prep time: 10 minutes | **Cook time:** 35 minutes | **Serves** 2

- 1 whole sea bass (1.5–2 pounds, head and tail intact, cleaned)
- 1-inch piece of fresh ginger, peeled and coarsely chopped
- 5 cloves garlic, peeled and coarsely chopped
- 2 tablespoons olive oil or vegetable oil
- 1/2 teaspoon black mustard seeds
- 2 whole dried red peppers (optional)
- 1/2 teaspoon ground turmeric
- 1 cup chopped cilantro
- 2 tablespoons lemon juice
- 1/2 teaspoon salt

1. Rinse the fish thoroughly under cold running water and pat dry inside and out. Preheat the oven to 400°F.
2. In a blender, combine the ginger, garlic, and 3 tablespoons of water. Blend on high until smooth.
3. Heat oil in a skillet (8–10 inches) over medium-high heat. Add the mustard seeds and allow them to pop, then add the red peppers and stir briefly. Pour in the blended paste, add turmeric, and stir-fry for about 2 minutes.
4. Transfer the skillet contents back to the blender. Add the cilantro, lemon juice, and salt. Blend on high until smooth, adding up to 2 tablespoons of water if needed.
5. Line a large baking dish with heavy-duty aluminum foil. Coat the fish inside and out with the green chutney paste. Wrap the fish completely in the foil.
6. Bake for 30 minutes. Serve hot.

EASY FISH CURRY

Prep time: 10 minutes | **Cook time:** 20 minutes | **Serves** 4

- 3 tablespoons canola oil
- ½ teaspoon mustard seeds
- 2 medium onions, finely sliced
- 4 garlic cloves, crushed
- 14 ounces cherry tomatoes, halved
- 1 teaspoon chili powder
- 1 teaspoon ground coriander
- 1 ½ teaspoons ground cumin
- 1 teaspoon salt
- ¾ cup hot water
- 1.25–1.75 pounds firm white fish (such as cod, pollock, or coley), skinned, boned, and cut into 1 ¾-inch cubes
- 1 lemon, quartered
- 1 ounce fresh cilantro, finely chopped

1. Heat the oil in a non-stick skillet with a lid over medium heat. Add the mustard seeds and stir-fry for a couple of minutes until they pop. Add the onions and garlic, cooking for about 8 minutes until golden and softened.
2. Add the cherry tomatoes, cover with the lid, and cook for 4–5 minutes, until the mixture forms a paste-like consistency.
3. Stir in the chili powder, ground coriander, ground cumin, salt, and hot water. Once the liquid begins to bubble, gently add the fish cubes. Stir carefully to coat, cover, and cook for 3–4 minutes, or until the fish is fully cooked.
4. Serve with rice, a generous squeeze of lemon, and a sprinkle of fresh cilantro.

CHAPTER 7: LENTILS AND BEANS

CURRIED MUNG BEANS

Prep time: 15 minutes | Cook time: 20 minutes | Serves 4

- 2 teaspoons coconut oil or safflower oil
- 1 teaspoon cumin seeds
- 4 garlic cloves, chopped
- 1 (1-inch) piece of ginger, chopped
- 1 tablespoon ground coriander
- 1 teaspoon garam masala
- ½–¾ teaspoon cayenne pepper
- ½ teaspoon ground turmeric
- 1 ½ cups chopped tomatoes
- 1 cup whole green mung beans, soaked for at least 1 hour
- 4 cups water
- 1–1 ½ teaspoons salt
- 1 cup coconut milk
- ¼ cup chopped cilantro, for garnish
- 1 teaspoon lemon juice, for garnish

1. Heat oil in a large skillet over medium heat. Add cumin seeds and cook for about 1 minute. Blend garlic, ginger, coriander, garam masala, cayenne, and turmeric with 2 tablespoons of water into a paste. Add to skillet and cook for 2 minutes until fragrant.
2. Blend tomatoes into a puree and add to the skillet. Cook for 5 minutes.
3. Stir in mung beans and water. Cover, bring to a boil, and cook for 6–8 minutes. Lower heat and simmer for 30–40 minutes, stirring halfway through, until mung beans are tender.
4. Add salt and coconut milk. Cover and cook for 10 minutes. Adjust seasoning if needed. Serve garnished with cilantro and lemon juice.

SIMPLE MARWARI-STYLE PEAS

Prep time: 10 minutes | Cook time: 10 minutes | Serves 4

- 2 tablespoons ghee, olive oil, peanut oil, or a mix of both
- 1/4 teaspoon whole cumin seeds
- 1 tablespoon fresh ginger, finely grated
- 1–2 fresh green chilies, finely chopped
- 2 1/3 cups peas (parboiled if fresh or thawed if frozen)
- 3/4 teaspoon salt
- Freshly ground black pepper

1. Heat ghee or oil in a non-stick skillet over medium heat. Add cumin seeds and let them sizzle for 10 seconds. Stir in ginger and chilies, cooking for 1 minute.
2. Add peas, salt, and pepper, stirring for 2–3 minutes. Sprinkle with a little water if the peas become too dry. Serve warm.

BUTTERNUT COCONUT RED LENTIL CURRY

Prep time: 20 minutes | **Cook time:** 20 minutes | **Serves** 4

- 2 teaspoons safflower or neutral oil
- ½ teaspoon black mustard seeds
- 8 curry leaves
- Pinch of asafoetida (optional for gluten-free)
- 2 garlic cloves, minced
- 1 ½ cups diced butternut squash, pumpkin, or other winter squash
- ¼ cup dried shredded coconut or fresh grated coconut
- ¼–½ teaspoon cayenne pepper
- ½ teaspoon garam masala
- ½ cup red lentils, washed and drained
- ½ cup coconut milk
- 1 ¼ cups water
- ¾ teaspoon salt, or to taste
- 1–2 teaspoons lemon juice, for garnish
- 2 tablespoons chopped cilantro, for garnish

1. Heat oil in a saucepan over medium heat. Add mustard seeds and curry leaves, cooking for 30 seconds. Stir in asafoetida (if using) and garlic, cooking until golden, about 1 minute.
2. Add squash and stir to coat. Cover and cook for 5 minutes. Mix in coconut, cayenne, and garam masala.
3. Add lentils, coconut milk, water, and salt. Stir well. Cover, bring to a boil, and cook for 7 minutes. Reduce heat to medium-low and cook for another 13–16 minutes, until the squash and lentils are tender.
4. Serve garnished with lemon juice and cilantro.

SOUTH INDIAN LENTILS WITH PUMPKIN

Prep time: 10 minutes | **Cook time:** 1 hour 15 minutes | **Serves** 4

- ½ cup toor dal (split pigeon peas), soaked in room-temperature water for 30 minutes, then washed and drained
- ½ cup pumpkin, deseeded and cut into 1-inch cubes (skin on)
- 2 tablespoons vegetable oil
- 1 teaspoon black mustard seeds
- 1 teaspoon cumin seeds
- 12 fresh or 15 dried curry leaves
- Large pinch of asafoetida
- 3 tablespoons tamarind pulp or store-bought tamarind paste
- 1 teaspoon sambhar powder
- ½ teaspoon ground turmeric
- 2 tablespoons chopped fresh cilantro, for garnish
- Salt, to taste
- Cooked rice, for serving

1. In a heavy-bottomed saucepan, combine lentils with double their volume of water. Bring to a boil over high heat, then reduce to a simmer. Cook for 50 minutes, skimming any foam and adding water as needed to keep the lentils submerged. When almost soft, add the pumpkin and cook for 15 minutes, allowing the lentils to become mushy.
2. Season with salt, stir, and set aside.
3. In a large saucepan, heat oil over high heat. Add mustard seeds and allow them to crackle. Add cumin seeds, curry leaves, and asafoetida, stirring briefly. Mix in tamarind pulp and cook over low heat for 4–5 minutes until thick, adding a splash of water to prevent drying out.
4. Serve the lentils topped with the tamarind mixture and garnish with cilantro. Pair with rice.

BLACK-EYED BEAN & MUSHROOM CURRY

Prep time: 10 minutes | **Cook time:** 55 minutes | **Serves** 4

- 2 tbsp. canola oil
- 2 onions, finely chopped
- 2 garlic cloves, grated
- 1-inch piece of fresh ginger, peeled and grated
- 14 oz can chopped tomatoes
- 1 tsp. salt
- 1 tsp. chili powder
- 1 tsp. garam masala
- 1 tsp. ground turmeric
- 10½ oz cremini mushrooms, sliced
- 1 cup canned coconut milk
- 14 oz can black-eyed beans, drained and rinsed

1. Heat the oil in a pan, add the onions, and cook over medium-low heat for 5 minutes until softened and lightly golden. Add the garlic and ginger, cooking for another minute.
2. Add the tomatoes and cook for 5 minutes, stirring occasionally.
3. Stir in the salt and spices, followed by the mushrooms, coconut milk, and black-eyed beans. Mix well and bring to a boil. Cover and simmer over medium heat for 15 minutes. (For a deeper flavor, cook on low heat for 30-40 minutes.) Serve warm.

RED KIDNEY BEAN & POTATO CURRY

Prep time: 10 minutes | **Cook time:** 50 minutes | **Serves** 4

- 2 tbsp. vegetable oil
- 1 tsp. cumin seeds
- 10 fresh curry leaves (optional)
- 2 onions, finely chopped
- 2 garlic cloves, grated
- 1-inch piece of fresh ginger, peeled and grated
- 2 tomatoes, finely chopped
- 1 tsp. salt
- 1 tsp. garam masala
- 1 tsp. chili powder
- 1 tsp. ground turmeric
- 2 tsp. ground coriander
- 1 large potato, peeled and cut into 1-inch cubes
- 14 oz can red kidney beans, drained and rinsed
- 2 cups boiling water
- Fresh cilantro, chopped, for garnish

1. Heat the oil in a pan, then add the cumin seeds and curry leaves. Once they sizzle, add the onions and cook for 6 minutes until golden. Add garlic and ginger and cook for another minute.
2. Stir in the tomatoes and cook for 5 minutes.
3. Add the salt, ground spices, potato, and beans, followed by boiling water. Mix well, cover, and cook for 15 minutes, stirring halfway through. (For richer flavor, cook on low heat for 30-40 minutes.) Garnish with fresh cilantro and serve.

DAILY DAL

Prep time: 10 minutes | Cook time: 30 minutes | Serves 4

- 8 oz red lentils
- 2 tbsp. canola oil
- Optional: 12 peppercorns
- Optional: 4 cloves
- 1 onion, thinly sliced
- 4 garlic cloves, crushed
- 2½-inch piece of ginger, peeled and finely grated
- ½ tsp. chili powder
- ½ tsp. ground coriander
- ½ tsp. ground turmeric
- 1 tsp. salt
- 11 oz canned plum tomatoes

1. Rinse the lentils in a sieve until the water runs clear. Place them in a deep saucepan, add 2½ cups of cold water, and bring to a boil over medium-high heat. Cover, reduce the heat, and simmer for 10-15 minutes until tender.
2. In another saucepan, heat the oil over medium heat. If using, add the peppercorns and cloves, stirring for about 1 minute until fragrant. Add the onions and cook for 8-10 minutes until golden.
3. Add the garlic and ginger, cooking for 4 minutes. Stir in the spices and salt. Add the tomatoes and simmer, covered, for 8 minutes.
4. Once the tomatoes have reduced, add the cooked lentils along with their water. Stir well and cook on low for 10 more minutes. Adjust salt and spice levels to taste. Serve with rice or flatbread.

SWEET VAL BEANS

Prep time: 10 minutes | Cook time: 40 minutes | Serves 4

- 1 tbsp. vegetable oil
- 1 tsp. black mustard seeds
- 1 tsp. cumin seeds
- Large pinch of asafoetida
- 10 fresh or 15 dried curry leaves
- 1 cup val beans (soaked for 8 hours, sprouted overnight, and skinned)
- 1 tsp. ground turmeric
- ½ tsp. medium-hot red chili powder
- 1 tsp. ground coriander
- 2 tbsp. grated jaggery or soft brown sugar
- 4 kokum petals or 2 tsp. lemon juice
- 2 tbsp. chopped fresh cilantro
- Salt, to taste

1. Heat the oil in a pan over high heat. Add mustard seeds and wait for them to pop. Then add cumin seeds, asafoetida, and curry leaves. Be cautious if using fresh curry leaves, as they may splutter.
2. Add the skinned val beans, followed by ground spices, jaggery (or sugar), salt, and enough water to cover the beans. Stir in the kokum or lemon juice.
3. Bring to a boil, then reduce the heat and simmer, covered, for 30 minutes or until the beans are tender. Add more water as needed. If you prefer a dry dish, uncover and cook over high heat until the liquid evaporates. Season to taste, and garnish with cilantro before serving.

GOAN BLACK-EYED PEAS WITH COCONUT

Prep time: 10 minutes | **Cook time: 1 hour 20 minutes** | **Serves 6**

- 2¼ cups dried black-eyed peas, washed and soaked overnight
- 3 medium onions, peeled
- 1 cup fresh grated coconut (or defrosted if frozen)
- 5 tbsp. olive oil or peanut oil
- 4–5 medium tomatoes (about 1½ lbs), peeled and finely chopped
- ¾–1 tsp. red chili powder
- 2 tbsp. ground coriander
- ¾ tsp. ground turmeric
- 2 tsp. salt, or to taste
- 2 tsp. garam masala

1. Drain the soaked peas and place them in a large pot with 6 cups of water. Bring to a boil, skimming off the froth that rises to the top. Partially cover the pot, reduce the heat, and simmer gently for 45–60 minutes, until the peas are tender. Once cooked, transfer the peas to a bowl and set aside. Wash the pot to remove any residue.

2. While the peas are cooking, finely chop one onion and place it in a blender with the grated coconut and ¾ cup water. Blend until you have a smooth paste, scraping down the sides as necessary. Set aside.

3. Finely chop the remaining onions. Heat the oil in the clean pot over medium-high heat. Once hot, add the onions and cook, stirring occasionally, until they brown around the edges. Add the chopped tomatoes and cook until they soften and break down into a thick paste, with the oil separating at the edges.

4. Add the coconut paste to the pot, stirring well and scraping any browned bits off the bottom of the pot. Stir in the chili powder, ground coriander, and turmeric, cooking for 7–8 minutes over medium heat until the mixture becomes fragrant and slightly browned.

5. Add the cooked black-eyed peas and their liquid to the pot, along with 4–8 tbsp. of water depending on your desired consistency. Stir in the salt and garam masala, bringing the mixture to a simmer. Cook, uncovered, for an additional 15–20 minutes or until the peas are very tender. Stir occasionally, adding more water if needed to reach your preferred thickness.

43

CHAPTER 8:
VEGETABLES, SALADS
AND PICKLES

CARROT SALAD WITH PEANUTS

Prep time: 10 minutes | **Cook time:** 10 minutes | **Serves** 4–6

- 3 large carrots (about 15 oz), peeled and grated
- 1 tbsp. lime or lemon juice
- ½ tsp. sugar
- ½ tsp. salt
- 1 fresh hot green chili, finely chopped
- 3 tbsp. chopped fresh cilantro
- 4–5 tbsp. roasted peanuts, crushed
- 1 tsp. olive oil or peanut oil
- ½ tsp. whole brown mustard seeds
- 2 tbsp. golden raisins (optional)

1. In a large bowl, combine the grated carrots, lime juice, sugar, salt, chopped chili, cilantro, and crushed peanuts.
2. In a small frying pan, heat the oil over medium-high heat. When hot, add the mustard seeds. Once they pop (in a few seconds), add the golden raisins (if using). Immediately pour the hot oil mixture over the carrot salad and stir well. Taste and adjust seasoning as needed.

SWEET AND SOUR PUMPKIN

Prep time: 20 minutes | **Cook time:** 15 minutes | **Serves** 4

- 2 tsp. safflower oil or another neutral oil
- 1 tsp. mustard seeds
- 1 tsp. cumin seeds
- ¼ tsp. fenugreek seeds
- 5 cups diced peeled and seeded pumpkin or butternut squash
- 1 tsp. ground coriander
- 1 tsp. garam masala
- ½ to ¾ tsp. salt
- ¼ tsp. ground turmeric
- ¼ to ½ tsp. cayenne pepper
- 1 to 2 tbsp. sugar
- 1 tbsp. dry mango powder or 2 tsp. lemon juice
- ½ tsp. chaat masala, for garnish

1. Heat the oil in a skillet over medium heat. Once hot, add the mustard seeds, cumin seeds, and fenugreek seeds. Cook until fragrant, about 1 minute. Add the diced pumpkin and stir well to coat. Cover and cook for 10 minutes.
2. Stir in the ground coriander, garam masala, salt, turmeric, cayenne, sugar, and dry mango powder. Mix well. Reduce the heat to medium-low, cover, and cook for another 20–25 minutes, or until the pumpkin is tender. Stir occasionally, adding a splash of water if needed to prevent sticking.
3. Garnish with chaat masala and serve.

CARROT "WATER" PICKLE

Prep time: 10 minutes | Cook time: 20 minutes | Makes about 2 jars

- 11/3 tbsp. salt
- 4 tbsp. black mustard seeds
- 1½ pounds carrots
- 2 medium-sized beets
- 2 hot dried red peppers

1. Bring 4½ quarts of water and salt to a boil in a large pot.
2. Meanwhile, crush, pound, or grind the mustard seeds coarsely until they split at least in half, using a heavy mortar and pestle or an Indian grinding stone.
3. Peel the carrots, removing the green tops, and quarter them lengthwise. Halve each piece lengthwise once again.
4. Peel the beets and cut each into 3 rounds.
5. Place the beets and carrots in a clean 5–6-quart wide-mouthed jar. Pour the boiling salted water over them. Add the mustard seeds and the red peppers. Allow to cool. Stir and cover.
6. Put a small label with the date on it so you will remember when you started the pickle. Stir once a day for 7 days with a clean wooden spoon. Keep covered. The pickle should be ready by the seventh day.

STIR-FRIED CABBAGE

Prep time: 10 minutes | Cook time: 10 minutes | Serves 6

- 1 small green cabbage (about 1½ lbs)
- 1–3 fresh hot green chilies, finely chopped
- 2½ tbsp. olive or peanut oil
- ¾ tsp. whole brown mustard seeds
- 7–8 fresh curry leaves, lightly crushed in your hand
- 1–1¼ tsp. salt
- 3–4 tsp. lemon juice

1. Remove the damaged outer leaves of the cabbage. Quarter it lengthwise and remove the hard core. Shred or slice the cabbage into slivers about ⅛ inch thick. You should have about 1¼ lbs. Place in a bowl and add the green chilies.
2. Heat oil in a wok or large pan over medium heat. Once hot, add the mustard seeds. When they pop, add the curry leaves (take care, as they may splutter), then quickly add the cabbage mixture. Stir-fry until the cabbage wilts, about 2–3 minutes.
3. Lower the heat, then add salt and lemon juice. Stir thoroughly, and turn off the heat. The cabbage should be wilted but still crunchy. Taste and adjust seasoning if needed.

SIMPLE TWICE-COOKED EGGPLANT

Prep time: 10 minutes | **Cook time:** 20 minutes | **Serves** 3–4

- 2 lbs eggplants (about 3 medium purple ones)
- 4 tbsp. olive, peanut, or mustard oil
- ½ tsp. whole cumin seeds
- ½ tsp. whole fennel seeds
- ¼ tsp. nigella seeds (kalonji)
- 1 large onion (7–8 oz), peeled and finely chopped
- 3-inch piece of fresh ginger, peeled and finely chopped
- 3 large garlic cloves, peeled and finely chopped
- 1–2 fresh hot green chilies, finely chopped
- 2 good-sized tomatoes (about ¾ lb), peeled and finely chopped
- 1 tsp. salt
- 3 tbsp. chopped fresh cilantro

1. Preheat the oven to 400°F.
2. Using a fork, prick the eggplants all over. Place them in a roasting pan in the oven for 1¼ hours, or until tender. Peel the eggplants and chop them finely.
3. Heat oil in a non-stick wok or frying pan over medium-high heat. When hot, add the cumin seeds. Let them sizzle for 3–4 seconds, then add the fennel and nigella seeds. After 2 seconds, add the onions, stirring and sautéing for 5–6 minutes until just starting to brown.
4. Add the ginger, garlic, and green chilies. Stir and cook for 2 minutes. Add the tomatoes and cook for 5–6 minutes until they soften.
5. Add the eggplant and salt, and cook for 5 minutes. Stir in the cilantro and cook for another 3 minutes.

GREEN BEAN SALAD

Prep time: 10 minutes | **Cook time:** 10 minutes | **Serves** 4

- 2¼ cups green beans (round or flat), cut crosswise into ¼-inch pieces
- 3 tbsp. peeled and finely chopped shallots
- 1–3 fresh hot green chilies, very finely chopped
- 4 tbsp. freshly grated coconut, or defrosted if frozen
- 2 tbsp. chopped fresh cilantro
- ½ tsp. salt, or to taste
- 1 tsp. olive or peanut oil
- ½ tsp. whole brown mustard seeds
- 1 tbsp. lime juice

1. Steam the beans for about 10 minutes, until tender but still crisp. (You could also parboil and drain them.) Refresh with cold water, then pat dry. Place in a bowl and mix in the shallots, green chilies, coconut, cilantro, and salt.
2. Heat the oil in a small frying pan over medium-high heat. When hot, add the mustard seeds. As soon as they pop, pour the oil and seeds over the beans. Stir to mix.
3. Add the lime juice just before serving and toss again.

SPINACH WITH POTATOES

Prep time: 10 minutes | **Cook time:** 40 minutes | **Serves** 4

- 2 tbsp. vegetable oil
- ½ tsp. cumin seeds
- 1 onion, finely chopped
- 1 fresh green chili, diced
- 1 tsp. ginger-garlic paste
- 1 tomato, finely chopped
- 1 tsp. garam masala
- 2 potatoes, peeled and cubed
- 2½ cups fresh spinach, washed, drained, and finely chopped
- Salt

1. Heat the oil in a heavy-based pan over high heat, add the cumin seeds, and fry for 10 seconds until they darken. Add the onion and chili and fry for 5–6 minutes until softened.
2. Stir in the ginger-garlic paste and tomato, and cook over low heat for 2–3 minutes until the tomato becomes mushy.
3. Add the garam masala and potatoes, then season with salt. Add enough water to barely cover the potatoes and bring to a boil. Reduce the heat and simmer for 25 minutes, until the potatoes are soft. Add the spinach, season to taste, heat through, and serve.

CARROTS AND PEAS WITH GINGER AND CILANTRO

Prep time: **10 minutes** | **Cook time:** **30 minutes** | **Serves** **4–6**

- A piece of fresh ginger, 2 inches by 1 inch, peeled and coarsely chopped
- 1½ pounds young, slim carrots
- 6 tbsp. vegetable oil
- ¼ tsp. whole black mustard seeds
- 5 whole fenugreek seeds
- ¼ tsp. ground turmeric
- 1 packed cup coarsely chopped cilantro
- 1 fresh hot green chili, washed and finely sliced (optional, or substitute ¼ tsp. cayenne pepper)
- 1 pound fresh peas, shelled
- 1 tsp. ground coriander
- 1 tsp. ground cumin
- 1 tsp. garam masala
- 1 tsp. salt

1. Put the ginger in a blender with 3 tbsp. of water and blend until smooth (about one minute).
2. Peel the carrots and slice them into rounds about ⅛ inch thick.
3. Heat the oil in a 10–12-inch skillet over medium heat. When very hot, add the mustard and fenugreek seeds. When the mustard seeds begin to pop (10 to 20 seconds), add the ginger paste and turmeric, being careful to avoid the splatter. Fry for about 2 minutes, stirring frequently. Add the chopped cilantro and green chili (or cayenne), and cook, stirring, for another 2 minutes. Add the carrots and peas, and cook for 5 more minutes, stirring frequently.
4. Add the coriander, cumin, garam masala, salt, and 3 tbsp. of warm water. Stir for a minute, cover, lower heat, and cook slowly for 30 minutes, stirring gently every 10 minutes or so.

CHAPTER 9: SNACKS AND STREET FOOD

SPICY PANEER SLICES

Prep time: 10 minutes | **Cook time:** 20 minutes | **Serves** 4

- 12 oz fresh Indian cheese (paneer), defrosted if frozen
- Scant ½ tsp salt
- ½–1 tsp red chili powder
- Scant ½ tsp ground turmeric
- 1 tbsp rice flour (rice powder)
- 1 tbsp chickpea flour (besan or gram flour)
- Oil, for frying
- Sprinkle of chaat masala (optional)

1. Cut paneer into slices about 1½ inches square and ½ inch thick.
2. Lay slices in a single layer. Dust one side with half the salt, chili powder, and turmeric. Rub evenly. Flip and repeat on the other side.
3. Combine rice flour and chickpea flour in a small bowl. Dip each paneer slice in the flour mixture, shaking off excess. Repeat with remaining slices. Cover and refrigerate for up to an hour if desired.
4. Heat ½ inch of oil in a medium pan over medium heat. Fry half the slices for about a minute on each side, until golden brown. Remove with a slotted spoon and drain on paper towels. Repeat with remaining slices.
5. Lightly sprinkle with chaat masala, if desired, and serve immediately.

MASALA CHICKEN WINGS

Prep time: 10 minutes | **Cook time:** 20 minutes | **Serves** 4

- 1 tsp ginger-garlic paste
- 1 tsp medium-hot red chili powder
- 1 tbsp ground cumin
- 2 cups chicken wings, skinned
- Vegetable oil, for deep-frying
- 3 tbsp cornstarch
- Salt

1. Combine ginger-garlic paste, chili powder, cumin, and salt in a bowl. Add the wings, coat in the marinade, cover, and marinate for at least 30 minutes (or overnight in the fridge).
2. Heat oil for deep frying in a pan. Once very hot, dip each wing in cornstarch, ensuring it's evenly coated. Deep fry in batches for 6–7 minutes, ensuring the chicken is cooked through (cut one open to check).
3. Remove wings with a slotted spoon and drain on paper towels. Serve hot.

CHILI CHEESE TOAST

Prep time: 10 minutes | **Cook time:** 15 minutes | **Serves** 4

- 2 to 3 tsp finely chopped serrano or jalapeño
- 3 scallions (white and green parts), finely chopped (about ⅓ cup)
- 2 generous cups grated white cheddar
- Freshly ground black pepper
- 2 tbsp salted butter, at room temperature
- 1 large garlic clove, finely minced (about 2 tsp)
- 4 (4 × 4-inch) slices sandwich bread
- Dried red chili flakes, for garnish

1. Preheat the broiler and set the top rack 4 to 5 inches below the heat.
2. In a medium bowl, combine the green chili, scallions, cheese, and black pepper. Mix well and set aside.
3. In a small bowl, combine soft butter with garlic and blend well.
4. Spread half of the garlic butter on one side of each slice of bread. Place bread slices on a baking sheet, buttered-side up, and broil for about 2 minutes until golden brown.
5. Flip the bread, spread the remaining garlic butter on the other side, and broil until golden.
6. Divide the cheese mixture among the bread slices, pressing gently into the bread, then broil until bubbly, about 2 minutes.
7. Remove from the oven, cut diagonally, sprinkle with red chili flakes, and serve immediately.

CARROT HALVA

Prep time: **10 minutes** | **Cook time:** **1 hour 40 minutes** | **Serves** **4**

- 12 oz carrots
- ¼ cup water
- ¼ tsp ground cardamom or 3 whole cardamoms, crushed
- A pinch of saffron
- 1 cup milk
- 2 oz sugar
- 1 tsp melted unsalted butter or ghee
- 1 oz almonds (skinless)

1. Peel and grate the carrots.
2. In a large pan, mix the grated carrots, water, cardamom, and saffron. Bring to a boil, then reduce the heat. Cover the pan and simmer gently for about 1 hour, stirring every 10–15 minutes.
3. Add the milk and sugar, and simmer for a further 1 hour on low heat.
4. Add the butter or ghee and cook gently to evaporate the milk. This will take around 15 minutes, leaving minimal liquid in the carrots.
5. Transfer to a serving dish and decorate with almonds. Serve either hot or cold.

CARAMELIZED BANANAS WITH SESAME SEEDS

Prep time: **10 minutes** | **Cook time:** **10 minutes** | **Serves** **2–4**

- 1 tsp sesame seeds
- 2 tbsp ghee (clarified butter) or ordinary butter
- 2 tbsp sugar
- 2 ripe but firm bananas
- ½ cup heavy cream, lightly whipped to soft peaks (optional)

1. Heat a small cast-iron frying pan over medium heat. Add the sesame seeds and toast them, stirring constantly for about 1 minute until they darken slightly and become fragrant. Transfer to a small bowl. (You can do this ahead of time.)
2. Melt the ghee or butter in a medium nonstick frying pan over low heat. Sprinkle in the sugar and stir to help it caramelize. Peel the bananas, cut them in half crosswise, then lengthwise. Arrange the bananas in a single layer in the pan and cook over medium-low heat for about 1½ minutes per side until golden and caramelized.
3. Transfer the bananas to a serving dish, sprinkle the sesame seeds over them, and serve hot, offering whipped cream separately, if desired.

MASALA CHIPS

Prep time: 5 minutes | **Cook time:** 20 minutes | **Serves** 4

- 2 lb frozen chips (preferably deep-fry, but oven-baked will work)
- Rapeseed (canola) oil, for deep-frying
- 1 tsp red chili powder
- ½ tsp ground cumin
- 1 tsp ground coriander
- Salt, to taste
- 2 tbsp rapeseed (canola) oil
- 1 tbsp cumin seeds
- 5 tbsp tomato hamburger relish
- 5 tbsp tomato ketchup
- 1 tbsp sugar
- ½ onion, finely chopped
- 1 tbsp garlic and ginger paste

1. Make the sauce: Heat oil in a saucepan over medium-high heat. Add cumin seeds and sauté for 30 seconds until fragrant. Stir in hamburger relish and ketchup, bringing to a simmer. Add sugar and cook for 1 minute, then stir in the chopped onion and garlic-ginger paste. Season with salt and set aside.

2. Cook the chips according to package instructions. If using frozen chips, deep fry them for the best results, or bake for a lighter option. Once cooked, season the chips with red chili powder, cumin, coriander, and salt (consider the saltiness of the sauce).

3. While the chips are still hot, toss them in the sauce, ensuring each chip is coated. Serve immediately for the crispiest, most flavorful masala chips.

BLACK GRAM FRITTERS

Prep time: 4 hours or overnight + 15 minutes | **Cook time:** 20 minutes | **Serves** 4

- 1 cup split black gram (urad dal), soaked in 3 cups of water for 4 hours or overnight, rinsed and drained
- ½ tsp cumin seeds
- 1 green chile, chopped (seeds removed to reduce heat)
- ½-inch knob of ginger
- Pinch of asafetida
- (optional, omit to make gluten-free)
- ¼ tsp freshly crushed black pepper (optional)
- 3 to 5 tbsp water
- 1 tsp salt, plus more if needed
- 1 tsp baking powder (only if baking)
- ¼ tsp baking soda (only if baking)

1. Grind the soaked black gram in a wet grinder or food processor for 1 minute. Add cumin, chile, ginger, asafetida, black pepper (if using), and salt. Grind in bursts of 30 seconds, adding water gradually to form a thick, fluffy mixture (3–4 minutes). Use a spatula to move the mixture between bursts. The batter should be thick, fluffy, and slightly gritty.

2. To check the aeration, drop a teaspoon of batter into a cup of water; it should float. If it doesn't, stir the batter briskly for 1 minute to aerate it.

3. To fry the vadas, heat about 2 inches of oil in a skillet over medium heat. Dip an ice cream scoop or wet hand into the batter, and carefully drop it into the hot oil. Fry the fritters in batches for 2–4 minutes per side, or until golden brown. Remove with a slotted spoon and drain on paper towels. Serve warm with sambhar and coconut chutney.

BEET AND FETA SAMOSAS

Prep time: 10 minutes | Cook time: 1 hour 10 minutes | Makes 18 to 24 samosas

- 14 oz fresh beets
- 7 oz feta cheese, cut into ¼-inch cubes
- 4 scallions, finely chopped
- 1 medium bunch of cilantro (1 ounce), finely chopped
- 1 fresh green chili, finely chopped
- 4 cloves garlic, crushed
- ½ tsp chili powder
- 1 tsp toasted cumin seeds, crushed
- 1 tsp garam masala
- ¾ tsp salt (or to taste)

1. Boil the beets until tender (about 1 hour). Test with a knife to ensure they're fully cooked. For a shortcut, you can use pre-cooked beets, though the flavor may not be as rich.

2. Drain the beets, cool under cold water, peel the skin, and mash roughly with a potato masher. Stir-fry the mash in a hot pan for 5 minutes to remove excess moisture. The mixture should be dry for crispy samosas. Transfer to a large bowl.

3. Add the feta cheese, scallions, cilantro, green chili, garlic, chili powder, cumin, garam masala, and salt. Taste and adjust the seasoning as needed. Ensure it is packed with flavor, as it will mellow inside the filo dough.

ONION FRITTERS

Prep time: 10 minutes | Cook time: 25 minutes | Serves 4

- ½ tsp. medium-hot red chili powder
- Pinch of ajwain seeds
- ½ cup chickpea flour (gram flour)
- 2 medium onions, thinly sliced
- Vegetable oil, for deep-frying
- Salt, to taste
- Coriander and Peanut Chutney or Sweet Tamarind Chutney, for serving

1. In a bowl, combine chili powder, salt, ajwain seeds, and chickpea flour. Add enough water to create a thick, custard-like batter. Fold in some onions, coating them evenly with the spice mixture. The batter's consistency should resemble that for Pakoras. It's best to add small batches of onions at a time to prevent the salt from drawing out too much moisture.

2. Heat enough oil in a deep frying pan to hold a single layer of fritters over high heat. Test the oil temperature by dropping in a slice of onion—the oil should sizzle. Fry the mixture in batches, dropping spoonfuls of batter into the pan, leaving space to flip the fritters. Fry for 3–4 minutes until golden, then flip and cook for another couple of minutes. Transfer to paper towels to drain. Serve immediately with coriander and peanut chutney or sweet tamarind chutney.

POTATO QUINOA PATTIES

Prep time: 45 minutes | **Cook time:** 20 minutes | **Makes** 10 patties

- 3 medium potatoes, boiled, peeled, and mashed
- 1 ½ cups cooked quinoa (about ½ cup uncooked)
- ¾ cup finely chopped red or white onion
- 1 to 2 hot green chilies, finely chopped (remove seeds for less heat)
- ¼ cup packed chopped cilantro
- 1 tbsp. minced or grated ginger
- ½ to ¾ tsp. carom seeds or cumin seeds
- ½ tsp. cayenne pepper
- 1 tsp. ground coriander
- ¼ tsp. black salt (or regular salt)
- ¾ tsp. salt, or to taste
- 1 tsp. safflower oil (or other neutral oil)
- ¼ cup or more breadcrumbs
- Safflower oil, as needed

1. In a large bowl, combine the mashed potatoes and cooked quinoa. Mash well to combine.
2. Add the onion, chilies, cilantro, ginger, carom seeds, cayenne pepper, coriander, black salt, and regular salt. Mix well, taste, and adjust seasonings as needed. If the mixture is too wet, add breadcrumbs to help shape the patties.
3. Form 3-inch patties by hand or with a cookie cutter.
4. Heat 1 tsp. of oil in a large skillet over medium-high heat. Tilt the pan to spread the oil. Place the patties in the skillet, making sure they don't touch. Cook for 6–8 minutes on each side until golden brown. Remove from the skillet and set aside. Repeat with the remaining patties.
5. Preheat the oven to 425°F. Place the patties on a parchment-lined baking sheet. Lightly brush with oil. Bake for 15 minutes, then broil for 2 minutes. Flip the patties, lightly brush or spray with oil, and broil for another 2 minutes.

CHAPTER 10: DRINKS AND DESSERTS

STEWED DRIED APRICOTS WITH CARDAMOM

Prep time: **10 minutes** | **Cook time:** **35 minutes** | **Serves** 4

- 1 cup Indian Hunza apricots or organic dried apricots
- ½ cup caster sugar
- 4 tbsp. heavy cream
- 1 tbsp. flaked almonds, for garnish
- 1 tbsp. crushed pistachios, for garnish
- 4 green cardamom pods, seeds crushed and husks discarded, for garnish

1. Place the apricots and sugar in a heavy-based saucepan, adding enough water to just cover the fruit. Bring to a boil, then reduce the heat and cook for 30 minutes until the apricots are tender and pulpy. If the mixture dries out, add a splash of water. Remove from heat and remove the pits from the apricots (if using Hunza apricots).
2. Put half the apricots into a blender and pulse a few times until they resemble jam.
3. Spoon some whole apricots and some of the jam into four stemmed serving glasses. Allow to cool. Drizzle with the cream and garnish with almonds, pistachios, and crushed cardamom seeds. Serve chilled.

GINGER MINT TEA

Prep time: **10 minutes** | **Cook time:** **20 minutes** | **Serves** 4

- 3-inch piece of fresh ginger, peeled and sliced into thin rounds
- 20 fresh mint leaves
- Honey, preferably raw, for serving

1. Place the ginger and 4 cups water in a saucepan and bring to a boil. Reduce heat and simmer gently for 15–20 minutes, then strain into a warmed teapot. Discard the ginger.
2. Gently crush the mint leaves in your hand and add them to the teapot. Cover and steep for 5 minutes. Serve the tea with honey.

MELON BALLS WITH MINT

Prep time: 10 minutes | **Cook time: 10 minutes** | **Serves 4–5**

- 1 large melon (about 3¾ lbs)
- 1 tsp. ground cardamom
- 6 tbsp. sugar
- About 35 fresh mint leaves, finely chopped
- 2 tbsp. lime juice
- 2–3 tsp. kewra water, rose water, or orange blossom water

1. Cut the melon in half and discard the seeds. Use a melon baller to scoop out the flesh and place it in a serving bowl. Sprinkle with cardamom and mix well.
2. Place the sugar in a small bowl, add the mint leaves, and rub them into the sugar with your fingers. Add the lime juice and your choice of fragrant water. Stir well and pour over the melon balls. Mix, cover, and refrigerate, stirring occasionally. Serve cold in small dishes with the juices.

SAFFRON CREAM FUDGE

Prep time: 10 minutes (+ 4 hour soak) | **Cook time: 15 minutes** | **Makes 10 or more**

- ½ cup cashews, soaked for 4 hours or overnight and drained
- 2 to 4 tbsp. almond milk
- ⅛ tsp. salt
- ¼ cup sugar
- ½ tsp. saffron (6 to 8 strands)
- 1 tsp. vegan butter or oil
- 2 drops lemon juice
- 1 drop vanilla extract
- ⅓ to ½ cup ground oats or oat flour
- 1 to 2 tbsp. all-purpose flour or 1 tbsp. cornstarch
- 1 to 2 tbsp. powdered sugar
- Almond or pistachio slivers, for garnish

1. Blend the cashews with 2 tbsp. almond milk into a smooth, thick cashew cream. Add more almond milk or use ½ cup thick cashew cream if necessary. Add salt, sugar, and saffron, then blend until smooth.
2. Transfer the cashew cream to a skillet over medium-low heat. Add the butter and cook, stirring often, until the mixture thickens to a custard consistency, about 3 to 5 minutes. Let it cool completely, then chill in the refrigerator for 15 minutes.
3. Stir in the lemon juice and vanilla extract. Gradually add the oat flour, 1 tbsp. at a time, mixing well. Add the all-purpose flour and stir until the mixture becomes a sticky, soft dough. Taste and add powdered sugar if needed.
4. Oil your hands and shape 1 tbsp. of the mixture into flat discs. Garnish with pistachio or almond slivers or dust with powdered sugar. Store at room temperature for the day or refrigerate for up to a week.

BENGAL BAKED CURD WITH TAMARIND BERRIES

Prep time: **10 minutes** | Cook time: 30 minutes| Serves 4

- 1 cup plus 2 tbsp. plain Greek yogurt
- ¾ cup plus 2 tbsp. sweetened condensed milk
- ½ cup plus 2 tbsp. heavy cream
- ¼ cup ground almonds
- 1 tbsp. unsalted butter
- Sugar, to taste
- ¾ lb mixed berries (e.g., raspberries, blueberries, and strawberries)
- 1 tsp. tamarind paste (or to taste)

1. Preheat the oven to 300°F.
2. Combine the yogurt, condensed milk, and heavy cream in a bowl and whisk until fully combined. Divide the mixture between ramekins.
3. Place the ramekins in a deep roasting pan and pour enough just-boiled water around them to reach two-thirds of the way up their sides. Bake for 25 minutes. Remove from the oven, allow to cool, and refrigerate for a couple of hours until set.
4. Once set, place the almonds, butter, and 1½ tsp. of sugar in a non-stick saucepan over medium heat. Stir constantly for a couple of minutes until the almonds brown and form large crumbs. Transfer to a bowl to cool.
5. To prepare the tamarind berries, cut larger berries (such as strawberries) to match the size of the smaller ones. Add them to a saucepan along with 2 tbsp. sugar, 3 tbsp. water, and the tamarind paste. Heat for 2 to 3 minutes until the berries soften. Taste and add more sugar if needed. Remove from heat.
6. Serve the berries warm or cold (chilled is preferred). To assemble, spoon the tamarind berries over the baked curd and sprinkle with the toasted almonds.

CASHEW AND MILK FUDGE

Prep time: **10 minutes** | **Cook time:** **30 minutes** | **Makes** **12 squares**

- 1 can sweetened condensed milk
- ¼ cup unsalted butter, plus 1 tsp. for greasing the dish
- 4 tbsp. unsalted cashew nuts, finely
- crushed
- 4 green cardamom pods, seeds finely crushed and husks discarded
- Edible silver foil, for decoration (optional)

1. Place the condensed milk in a heavy-based saucepan over low heat and cook for 10–15 minutes, stirring constantly, until the mixture thickens and begins to pull away from the sides of the pan. Stir in the butter, cashews, and cardamom, then remove from the heat. The mixture should easily move with the back of a wooden spoon.
2. Grease a flat dish with the extra butter. Pour the mixture into the dish and smooth the surface with a spatula.
3. Allow to cool and set for 2–3 hours, then cut into 2.5 cm squares or diamonds. Optionally, decorate with more crushed nuts and edible silver foil.

SAFFRON APPLE AND ALMOND PUDDING

Prep time: 10 minutes | Cook time: 20 minutes | Serves 4

- 1 lb eating apples
- 1 cup water
- 4 oz sugar
- A pinch of saffron
- 2 tsp cornstarch mixed with 2 tsp water
- 4 oz almonds, finely chopped

1. Peel the apples and remove the cores. Slice the apples into thin chip-shaped pieces.
2. In a pan, combine the apples, water, sugar, and saffron. Bring to a boil, then lower the heat, cover, and simmer for about 5 minutes.
3. Stir in the cornstarch-water mixture and cook for another 2 to 3 minutes until the mixture thickens.
4. Transfer the contents to a serving dish and garnish with the chopped almonds. Serve hot or cold, with cream or custard.

BLACK PEPPER ICE CREAM

Prep time: 10 minutes | Cook time: 40 minutes | Serves 6 to 8

- 1¼ cups whole milk
- 1½ tbsp. cracked black pepper
- 1¼ cups heavy cream
- 5 egg yolks (save the whites for another recipe)
- ½ cup sugar

1. Pour the milk into a saucepan, add the cracked black pepper, and heat gently until small bubbles appear around the edges, but the milk has not yet reached a boil. Remove from heat and stir in the cream. Let it infuse for 15 to 20 minutes.
2. In a mixing bowl, whisk the egg yolks and sugar until pale and fluffy. Slowly add the egg mixture into the cream mixture, whisking constantly.
3. Return the saucepan to low heat, stirring constantly until the mixture thickens to a custard consistency and coats the back of a spoon.
4. Remove from heat and let it cool. Strain through a fine-mesh sieve or muslin cloth to remove the pepper bits. Refrigerate for a few hours until cold.
5. Churn in an ice cream maker for about 20 minutes, or pour the mixture into a plastic container and freeze. If freezing without an ice cream maker, whisk vigorously every 30 minutes for 2 to 3 hours until fully frozen.

INDIAN SPICED MILK TEA

Prep time: 15 minutes | **Cook time:** 15 minutes | **Serves** 4

- 1½ cups water
- 2 to 3 tbsp raw sugar or other sweetener, to taste
- 3½ tsp loose tea (Loose black tea leaves for chai.)
- ¾ tsp chai masala
- 1 tsp grated fresh ginger (adjust to taste)
- 2 cups plain almond milk or another creamy nondairy milk

1. In a saucepan over medium heat, combine the water, sugar, tea leaves, chai masala, and ginger. Bring to a rolling boil, about 8 to 9 minutes.
2. Gradually pour in the almond milk and bring the mixture to just below a boil, about 8 to 10 minutes.
3. Strain the tea into cups and serve hot.

SPICED HOT CHOCOLATE

Prep time: 10 minutes | **Cook time:** 10 minutes | **Serves** 2 to 4

- 1¾ cups whole milk
- ⅔ cup light cream
- 1 bay leaf
- 2 cloves
- 1 cinnamon stick
- 4 oz dark chocolate
- 4 tsp sugar (or to taste)
- A few shavings of nutmeg

1. Pour the milk and cream into a saucepan with the bay leaf, cloves, and cinnamon stick. Heat until the mixture is nearly boiling.
2. Lower the heat and break the dark chocolate into the pan. Stir until the chocolate is melted, then add the sugar.
3. Remove the bay leaf, cloves, and cinnamon stick, and serve the hot chocolate immediately in 2 large mugs or 4 small cups. Garnish with a few shavings of nutmeg.

MEASUREMENT CONVERSION CHART

VOLUME EQUIVALENTS(DRY)

US STANDARD	METRIC (APPROXIMATE)
1/8 teaspoon	0.5 mL
1/4 teaspoon	1 mL
1/2 teaspoon	2 mL
3/4 teaspoon	4 mL
1 teaspoon	5 mL
1 tablespoon	15 mL
1/4 cup	59 mL
1/2 cup	118 mL
3/4 cup	177 mL
1 cup	235 mL
2 cups	475 mL
3 cups	700 mL
4 cups	1 L

VOLUME EQUIVALENTS(LIQUID)

US STANDARD	US STANDARD (OUNCES)	METRIC (APPROXIMATE)
2 tablespoons	1 fl.oz.	30 mL
1/4 cup	2 fl.oz.	60 mL
1/2 cup	4 fl.oz.	120 mL
1 cup	8 fl.oz.	240 mL
1 1/2 cup	12 fl.oz.	355 mL
2 cups or 1 pint	16 fl.oz.	475 mL
4 cups or 1 quart	32 fl.oz.	1 L
1 gallon	128 fl.oz.	4 L

TEMPERATURES EQUIVALENTS

FAHRENHEIT(F)	CELSIUS(C) (APPROXIMATE)
225 °F	107 °C
250 °F	120 °C
275 °F	135 °C
300 °F	150 °C
325 °F	160 °C
350 °F	180 °C
375 °F	190 °C
400 °F	205 °C
425 °F	220 °C
450 °F	235 °C
475 °F	245 °C
500 °F	260 °C

WEIGHT EQUIVALENTS

US STANDARD	METRIC (APPROXIMATE)
1 ounce	28 g
2 ounces	57 g
5 ounces	142 g
10 ounces	284 g
15 ounces	425 g
16 ounces (1 pound)	455 g
1.5 pounds	680 g
2 pounds	907 g

The Dirty Dozen and Clean Fifteen

The Environmental Working Group (EWG) is a nonprofit, nonpartisan organization dedicated to protecting human health and the environment Its mission is to empower people to live healthier lives in a healthier environment. This organization publishes an annual list of the twelve kinds of produce, in sequence, that have the highest amount of pesticide residue-the Dirty Dozen-as well as a list of the fifteen kinds ofproduce that have the least amount of pesticide residue-the Clean Fifteen.

THE DIRTY DOZEN	THE CLEAN FIFTEEN
• The 2016 Dirty Dozen includes the following produce. These are considered among the year's most important produce to buy organic:	• The least critical to buy organically are the Clean Fifteen list. The following are on the 2016 list:

THE DIRTY DOZEN

Strawberries	Spinach
Apples	Tomatoes
Nectarines	Bell peppers
Peaches	Cherry tomatoes
Celery	Cucumbers
Grapes	Kale/collard greens
Cherries	Hot peppers

• The Dirty Dozen list contains two additional itemskale/collard greens and hot peppers-because they tend to contain trace levels of highly hazardous pesticides.

THE CLEAN FIFTEEN

Avocados	Papayas
Corn	Kiw
Pineapples	Eggplant
Cabbage	Honeydew
Sweet peas	Grapefruit
Onions	Cantaloupe
Asparagus	Cauliflower
Mangos	

• Some of the sweet corn sold in the United States are made from genetically engineered (GE) seedstock. Buy organic varieties of these crops to avoid GE produce.

APPENDIX 3: INDEX

Hey there!

Wow, can you believe we've reached the end of this culinary journey together? I'm truly thrilled and filled with joy as I think back on all the recipes we've shared and the flavors we've discovered. This experience, blending a bit of tradition with our own unique twists, has been a journey of love for good food. And knowing you've been out there, giving these dishes a try, has made this adventure incredibly special to me.

Even though we're turning the last page of this book, I hope our conversation about all things delicious doesn't have to end. I cherish your thoughts, your experiments, and yes, even those moments when things didn't go as planned. Every piece of feedback you share is invaluable, helping to enrich this experience for us all.

I'd be so grateful if you could take a moment to share your thoughts with me, be it through a review on Amazon or any other place you feel comfortable expressing yourself online. Whether it's praise, constructive criticism, or even an idea for how we might do things differently in the future, your input is what truly makes this journey meaningful.

This book is a piece of my heart, offered to you with all the love and enthusiasm I have for cooking. But it's your engagement and your words that elevate it to something truly extraordinary.

Thank you from the bottom of my heart for being such an integral part of this culinary adventure. Your openness to trying new things and sharing your experiences has been the greatest gift.

Catch you later,

Cristi G. Piedra

Printed in Great Britain
by Amazon

53107214R00044